# Performance Testing
# with JMeter

*Second Edition*

Test web applications using Apache JMeter with
practical, hands-on examples

**Bayo Erinle**

BIRMINGHAM - MUMBAI

# Performance Testing with JMeter
## *Second Edition*

First published: July 2013

Second edition: April 2015

Production reference: 1200415

Published by Packt Publishing Ltd.
Livery Place
35 Livery Street
Birmingham B3 2PB, UK.

ISBN 978-1-78439-481-3

www.packtpub.com

# Credits

**Author**
Bayo Erinle

**Reviewers**
Vinay Madan
Satyajit Rai
Ripon Al Wasim

**Commissioning Editor**
Pramila Balan

**Acquisition Editor**
Llewellyn Rozario

**Content Development Editor**
Adrian Raposo

**Technical Editors**
Tanvi Bhatt
Narsimha Pai
Mahesh Rao

**Copy Editors**
Charlotte Carneiro
Pranjali Chury
Rashmi Sawant

**Project Coordinator**
Kinjal Bari

**Proofreaders**
Simran Bhogal
Safis Editing
Joanna McMahon

**Indexer**
Monica Ajmera Mehta

**Production Coordinator**
Arvindkumar Gupta

**Cover Work**
Arvindkumar Gupta

# About the Author

**Bayo Erinle** is an author and senior software engineer with over 11 years of experience in designing, developing, testing, and architecting software. He has worked in various spectrums of the IT field, including government, commercial, finance, and health care. As a result, he has been involved in the planning, development, implementation, integration, and testing of numerous applications, including multi-tiered, standalone, distributed, and cloud-based applications. He is passionate about programming, performance, scalability, and all things technical. He is always intrigued by new technology and enjoys learning new things.

He currently resides in Maryland, US, and when he is not hacking away at some new technology, he enjoys spending time with his wife, Nimota, and their three children, Mayowa, Durotimi, and Fisayo.

He also authored *Performance Testing with JMeter 2.9* (first edition) and *JMeter Cookbook,* both by *Packt Publishing*.

I'd like to thank my wife and children for the countless hours of sacrifice they endured while I worked on this project. I truly appreciate their help.

# About the Reviewers

**Vinay Madan** is a consultant QA analyst and has an MS degree in information systems. He has more than 8 years of experience in diversified fields of software testing, quality assurance, and test management, both manual and automated.

He has worked on projects for leading international clients on smart card issuance, payment gateway, big data, security, telecom, and e-learning. He is an avid learner with strong technical expertise on functional and performance automation testing tools, such as Selenium, QTP, Cucumber, JMeter, and Load Runner.

Over the years, he has worked with multiple testing methodologies, including Agile, Scrum and customized Waterfall for Windows, the Web, and mobile. He is passionate about automation, open source technologies and loves sharing his knowledge on blogs and forums.

**Satyajit Rai** is a programmer with an interest in the design and implementation of large-scale distributed systems. He has designed and developed large and complex enterprise systems as well Internet-scale systems. He has developed expertise on different programming languages on different platforms. He is passionate about development-related best practices and puts a lot of emphasis on the performance, reliability, maintainability, and operability aspects of the system.

Over the course of his work at Persistent Systems Ltd, Pune, India, he worked on the performance aspects of many systems at different stages, such as architecture, design, deployment, performance evaluation, and tuning. He used his knowledge of a diverse set of systems to improve the performance of many such systems. At Persistent Systems, he was also instrumental in building a large-scale performance testing service, which was developed using JMeter on the AWS cloud.

I would like to thank my wife, Minakshi, and son, Achintya, for being patient and allowing me to spend time on the review.

**Ripon Al Wasim** is currently a senior software engineer at Cefalo (http://www.cefalo.com/). He lives in Dhaka, Bangladesh. He has over 13 years of experience in the software industry. His professional expertise includes software development and testing. He also has some experience as a trainer in Java and testing.

He is a Sun Certified Java Programmer (SCJP) and JLPT Level 3 (Japanese Language Proficiency Test) certified.

Ripon is an active participant in the professional community Stack Overflow (http://stackoverflow.com/users/617450/ripon-al-wasim).

He is also one of the reviewers of *Selenium WebDriver Practical Guide*, Ripon's first official effort with *Packt Publishing*.

I would like to thank my mother, who always prays for me. I would like to extend deep gratitude and thanks to my wife, Koly, for her everlasting love and support. I like to play and simply enjoy with my daughter, Nawar, and my son, Nazif, in my leisure time. Thanks a lot to Mohammad Golam Kabir, cofounder of Cefalo, for his inspiration.

# www.PacktPub.com

## Support files, eBooks, discount offers, and more

For support files and downloads related to your book, please visit www.PacktPub.com.

Did you know that Packt offers eBook versions of every book published, with PDF and ePub files available? You can upgrade to the eBook version at www.PacktPub.com and as a print book customer, you are entitled to a discount on the eBook copy. Get in touch with us at service@packtpub.com for more details.

At www.PacktPub.com, you can also read a collection of free technical articles, sign up for a range of free newsletters and receive exclusive discounts and offers on Packt books and eBooks.

https://www2.packtpub.com/books/subscription/packtlib

Do you need instant solutions to your IT questions? PacktLib is Packt's online digital book library. Here, you can search, access, and read Packt's entire library of books.

## Why subscribe?

- Fully searchable across every book published by Packt
- Copy and paste, print, and bookmark content
- On demand and accessible via a web browser

## Free access for Packt account holders

If you have an account with Packt at www.PacktPub.com, you can use this to access PacktLib today and view 9 entirely free books. Simply use your login credentials for immediate access.

# Table of Contents

# Preface

Performance testing is a type of testing intended to determine the responsiveness, reliability, throughput, interoperability, and scalability of a system and/or application under a given workload. It is critical and essential to the success of any software product launch and its maintenance. It also plays an integral part in scaling an application out to support a wider user base.

Apache JMeter is a free open source, cross-platform, performance testing tool that has been around since the late 90s. It is mature, robust, portable, and highly extensible. It has a large user base and offers lots of plugins to aid testing.

This is a practical hands-on book that focuses on how to leverage Apache JMeter to meet your testing needs. It starts with a quick introduction on performance testing, but quickly moves into engaging topics, including recording test scripts, monitoring system resources, an extensive look at several JMeter components, leveraging the cloud for testing, extending Apache JMeter capabilities via plugins, and so on. Along the way, you will do some scripting, learn and use tools such as Vagrant, Apache Tomcat, and be armed with all the knowledge you need to take on your next testing engagement.

Whether you are a developer or tester, this book is sure to give you some valuable knowledge to aid you in attaining success in your future testing endeavors.

## What this book covers

*Chapter 1*, *Performance Testing Fundamentals*, covers the fundamentals of performance testing and the installation and configuration of JMeter.

*Chapter 2*, *Recording Your First Test*, dives into recording your first JMeter test script and covers the anatomy of a JMeter test script.

*Chapter 3, Submitting Forms*, covers form submission in detail. It includes handling various HTML form elements (checkboxes, radio, file uploads and downloads, and so on), JSON data, and XML.

*Chapter 4, Managing Sessions*, explains session management, including cookies and URL rewriting.

*Chapter 5, Resource Monitoring*, dives into the active monitoring of system resources while executing tests. You get to start up a server and extend JMeter via plugins.

*Chapter 6, Distributed Testing*, takes an in-depth look at leveraging the cloud for performance testing. We dive into tools such as Vagrant and AWS, and explore the existing cloud testing platforms, BlazeMeter and Flood.io.

*Chapter 7, Helpful Tips*, provides you with helpful techniques and tips for getting the most out of JMeter.

# What you need for this book

To successfully execute the code samples provided in this book, you need the following:

- A computer with an Internet connection
- Apache JMeter (`http://jmeter.apache.org/`)
- Java Runtime Environment (JRE) or Java Development Kit (JDK) (`http://www.oracle.com/technetwork/java/javase/downloads/index.html`)
- In addition, for *Chapter 5, Resource Monitoring*, you need the following:
    - Apache Tomcat (`http://tomcat.apache.org`)
- For *Chapter 6, Distributed Testing*, you need the following :
    - Vagrant (`http://www.vagrantup.com/`)
    - An AWS account (`http://aws.amazon.com/`)
    - A BlazeMeter account (`http://blazemeter.com/`)
    - A Flood.io account (`https://flood.io/`)

This book contains pointers and additional helpful links in setting all these up.

# Who this book is for

The book is targeted primarily at developers and testers. Developers who have always been intrigued by performance testing and have wanted to dive in on the action will find it extremely useful and gain insightful skills as they walk through the practical examples in this book.

Testers will also benefit from this book since it will guide them through solving practical, real-world challenges when testing modern web applications, giving them ample knowledge to aid them in becoming better testers. Additionally, they will be exposed to certain helpful testing tools that will come in handy at some point in their testing careers.

# Conventions

In this book, you will find a number of text styles that distinguish between different kinds of information. Here are some examples of these styles and an explanation of their meaning.

Code words in text, database table names, folder names, filenames, file extensions, pathnames, dummy URLs, user input, and Twitter handles are shown as follows: "Should you need to customize JMeter default values, you can do so by editing the jmeter.properties file in the JMETER_HOME/bin folder, or making a copy of that file, renaming it to something different (for example, my-jmeter.properties), and specifying that as a command-line option when starting JMeter."

A block of code is set as follows:

```
name=firstName0lastName0
name_g=2
name_g0="firstName":"Larry","jobs":[{"id":1,"description":"Doctor"}],"
lastName":"Ellison"
name_g1=Larry
name_g2=Ellison
server=jmeterbook.aws.af.cm
```

When we wish to draw your attention to a particular part of a code block, the relevant lines or items are set in bold:

```
name=firstName0lastName0
name_g=2
name_g0="firstName":"Larry","jobs":[{"id":1,"description":"Doctor"}],"
lastName":"Ellison"
name_g1=Larry
name_g2=Ellison
server=jmeterbook.aws.af.cm
```

Any command-line input or output is written as follows:

```
vagrant ssh n1
cd /opt/apache-jmeter-2.12/bin
./jmeter --version
```

**New terms** and **important words** are shown in bold. Words that you see on the screen, for example, in menus or dialog boxes, appear in the text like this: "Launch **JMeter**."

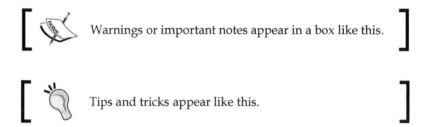

> Warnings or important notes appear in a box like this.

> Tips and tricks appear like this.

# Reader feedback

Feedback from our readers is always welcome. Let us know what you think about this book—what you liked or disliked. Reader feedback is important for us as it helps us develop titles that you will really get the most out of.

To send us general feedback, simply e-mail feedback@packtpub.com, and mention the book's title in the subject of your message.

If there is a topic that you have expertise in and you are interested in either writing or contributing to a book, see our author guide at www.packtpub.com/authors.

# Customer support

Now that you are the proud owner of a Packt book, we have a number of things to help you to get the most from your purchase.

# Downloading the example code

You can download the example code files from your account at http://www.packtpub.com for all the Packt Publishing books you have purchased. If you purchased this book elsewhere, you can visit http://www.packtpub.com/support and register to have the files e-mailed directly to you.

# Downloading the color images of this book

We also provide you with a PDF file that has color images of the screenshots/ diagrams used in this book. The color images will help you better understand the changes in the output. You can download this file from: `https://www.packtpub.com/sites/default/files/downloads/4813OS_ColoredImages.pdf`.

# Errata

Although we have taken every care to ensure the accuracy of our content, mistakes do happen. If you find a mistake in one of our books — maybe a mistake in the text or the code — we would be grateful if you could report this to us. By doing so, you can save other readers from frustration and help us improve subsequent versions of this book. If you find any errata, please report them by visiting `http://www.packtpub.com/submit-errata`, selecting your book, clicking on the **Errata Submission Form** link, and entering the details of your errata. Once your errata are verified, your submission will be accepted and the errata will be uploaded to our website or added to any list of existing errata under the Errata section of that title.

To view the previously submitted errata, go to `https://www.packtpub.com/books/content/support` and enter the name of the book in the search field. The required information will appear under the **Errata** section.

# Piracy

Piracy of copyrighted material on the Internet is an ongoing problem across all media. At Packt, we take the protection of our copyright and licenses very seriously. If you come across any illegal copies of our works in any form on the Internet, please provide us with the location address or website name immediately so that we can pursue a remedy.

Please contact us at `copyright@packtpub.com` with a link to the suspected pirated material.

We appreciate your help in protecting our authors and our ability to bring you valuable content.

# Questions

If you have a problem with any aspect of this book, you can contact us at `questions@packtpub.com`, and we will do our best to address the problem.

# 1
# Performance Testing Fundamentals

*Software performance testing is used to determine the speed or effectiveness of a computer, network, software program or device. This process can involve quantitative tests done in a lab, such as measuring the response time or the number of MIPS (millions of instructions per second) at which a system functions.*

*-Wikipedia*

Let's consider a case study. Baysoft Training Inc. is an emerging start-up company focused on redefining how software will help to get more people trained in various fields in the IT industry. The company achieves this goal by providing a suite of products, including online courses, on-site training, and off-site training. As such, one of their flagship products TrainBot, a web-based application is focused solely on registering individuals for courses of interest that will aid them in attaining career goals. Once registered, the client can then go on to take a series of interactive online courses.

# The incident

Up until recently, traffic on TrainBot was light as it was only opened to a handful of clients, since it was still in closed beta. Everything was fully operational and the application as a whole was very responsive. Just a few weeks ago, TrainBot was opened to the public and all is still good and dandy. To celebrate the launch and promote its online training courses, Baysoft Training Inc. recently offered 75 percent off on all the training courses. However, this promotional offer caused a sudden influx on TrainBot, far beyond what the company had anticipated. Web traffic shot up by 300 percent and suddenly things took a turn for the worse. Network resources weren't holding up well, server CPUs and memory were at 90-95 percent, and database servers weren't far behind due to high I/O and contention. As a result, most web requests began to get slower response times, making TrainBot totally unresponsive for most of its first-time clients. It didn't take too long after that, for the servers to crash and for the support lines to get flooded.

# The aftermath

It was a long night at the Baysoft Training Inc. corporate office. How did this happen? Could this have been avoided? Why was the application and system not able to handle the load? Why weren't adequate performance and stress tests conducted on the system and application? Was it an application problem, a system resource issue, or a combination of both? All these were questions that the management demanded answers to from the group of engineers, which comprised software developers, network and system engineers, Quality Assurance (QA) testers, and database administrators gathered in the WAR room. There sure was a lot of finger pointing and blame to go around the room. After a little brainstorming, it wasn't long before the group had to decide what needed to be done. The application and its system resources needed to undergo extensive and rigorous testing. This included all facets of the application and all supporting system resources including, but not limited to, infrastructure, network, database, servers, and load balancers. Such a test would help all involved parties discover exactly where the bottlenecks are and address them accordingly.

# Performance testing

Performance testing is a type of testing intended to determine the responsiveness, reliability, throughput, interoperability, and scalability of a system and/or application under a given workload. It could also be defined as a process of determining the speed or effectiveness of a computer, network, software application, or device. Testing can be conducted on software applications, system resources, targeted application components, databases, and a whole lot more. It normally involves an automated test suite as it allows easy repeatable simulations of a variety of normal, peak, and exceptional load conditions. Such forms of testing help to verify whether a system or application meets the specifications claimed by its vendor. The process can compare applications in terms of parameters such as speed, data transfer rate, throughput, bandwidth, efficiency, or reliability. Performance testing can also aid as a diagnostic tool in determining bottlenecks and single points of failures. It is often conducted in a controlled environment and in conjunction with stress testing; a process of determining the ability of a system or application to maintain a certain level of effectiveness under unfavorable conditions.

Why bother? Using Baysoft's case study, it should be obvious why companies bother and go through great lengths to conduct performance testing. The disaster could have been minimized, if not totally eradicated, if effective performance testing had been conducted on TrainBot prior to opening it up to the masses. As we go ahead in this chapter, we will continue to explore the many benefits of effective performance testing.

At a very high level, performance testing is almost always conducted to address one or more risks related to expenses, opportunity costs, continuity, and/or corporate reputation. Conducting such tests helps to give insights into software application release readiness, adequacy of network and system resources, infrastructure stability, and application scalability, to name a few. Gathering estimated performance characteristics of application and system resources prior to the launch helps address issues early and provides valuable feedback to stakeholders; helping them make key and strategic decisions.

Performance testing covers a whole lot of ground including areas such as:

- Assessing application and system production readiness
- Evaluating against performance criteria (for example, transactions per second, page views per day, registrations per day, and so on)
- Comparing performance characteristics of multiple systems or system configurations
- Identifying the source of performance bottlenecks

- Aiding with performance and system tuning
- Helping to identify system throughput levels
- Acting as a testing tool

Most of these areas are intertwined with each other, each aspect contributing to attaining the overall objectives of stakeholders. However, before jumping right in, let's take a moment to understand the following core activities in conducting performance tests:

- **Identifying acceptance criteria**: What is the acceptable performance of the various modules of the application under load? Specifically, identifying the response time, throughput, and resource utilization goals and constraints. How long should the end user wait before rendering a particular page? How long should the user wait to perform an operation? Response time is usually a user concern, throughput a business concern, and resource utilization a system concern. As such, response time, throughput, and resource utilization are key aspects of performance testing. Acceptance criteria are usually driven by stakeholders and it is important to continuously involve them as the testing progresses, as the criteria may need to be revised.

- **Identifying the test environment**: Becoming familiar with the physical test and production environments is crucial for a successful test run. Knowing things such as the hardware, software, and network configurations of the environment helps to derive an effective test plan and identify testing challenges from the outset. In most cases, these will be revisited and/or revised during the testing cycle.

- **Planning and designing tests**: Know the usage pattern of the application (if any), and come up with realistic usage scenarios including variability among the various scenarios. For example, if the application in question has a user registration module, how many users typically register for an account in a day? Do those registrations happen all at once, at the same time, or are they spaced out? How many people frequent the landing page of the application within an hour? Questions such as these help put things in perspective and design variations in the test plan. Having said that, there may be times where the application under test is new and so no usage pattern has been formed yet. At such times, stakeholders should be consulted to understand their business process and come up with as close to a realistic test plan as possible.

- **Preparing the test environment**: Configure the test environment, tools, and resources necessary to conduct the planned test scenarios. It is important to ensure that the test environment is instrumented for resource monitoring to help analyze results more efficiently. Depending on the company, a separate team might be responsible for setting up the test tools; while another team may be responsible for configuring other aspects such as resource monitoring. In other organizations, a single team may be responsible for setting up all aspects.

- **Preparing the test plan**: Using a test tool, record the planned test scenarios. There are numerous testing tools available, both free and commercial that do the job quite well, with each having their pros and cons.

  Such tools include HP Load Runner, NeoLoad, LoadUI, Gatling, WebLOAD, WAPT, Loadster, LoadImpact, Rational Performance Tester, Testing Anywhere, OpenSTA, Loadstorm, The Grinder, Apache Benchmark, HttpPerf, and so on. Some of these are commercial while others are not as mature or portable or extendable as JMeter. HP Load Runner, for example, is a bit pricey and limits the number of simulated threads to 250 without purchasing additional licenses. It does offer a much better graphical interface and monitoring capability though. Gatling is the new kid on the block, is free and looks rather promising. It is still in its infancy and aims to address some of the shortcomings of JMeter, including easier testing DSL (domain-specific language) versus JMeter's verbose XML, and better and more meaningful HTML reports, among others. Having said that, it still has only a tiny user base as compared to JMeter, and not everyone may be comfortable with building test plans in Scala, its language of choice. Programmers may find it more appealing.

  In this book, our tool of choice will be Apache JMeter to perform this step. This shouldn't be a surprise considering the title of the book.

- **Running the tests**: Once recorded, execute the test plans under light load and verify the correctness of the test scripts and output results. In cases where test or input data is fed into the scripts to simulate more realistic data (more on this in later chapters), also validate the test data. Another aspect to pay careful attention to during test plan execution is the server logs. This can be achieved through the resource monitoring agents set up to monitor the servers. It is paramount to watch for warnings and errors. A high rate of errors, for example, can be an indication that something is wrong with the test scripts, application under test, system resource, or a combination of all these.

- **Analyzing results, report, and retest**: Examine the results of each successive run and identify areas of bottleneck that need to be addressed. These could be related to system, database, or application. System-related bottlenecks may lead to infrastructure changes, such as increasing memory available to the application, reducing CPU consumption, increasing or decreasing thread pool sizes, revising database pool sizes, reconfiguring network settings, and so on. Database-related bottlenecks may lead to analyzing database I/O operations, top queries from the application under test, profiling SQL queries, introducing additional indexes, running statistics gathering, changing table page sizes and locks, and a lot more. Finally, application-related changes might lead to activities such as refactoring application components, reducing application memory consumption and database round trips, and so on. Once the identified bottlenecks are addressed, the test(s) should then be rerun and compared with previous runs. To help better track what change or group of changes resolved a particular bottleneck, it is vital that changes are applied in an orderly fashion, preferably one at a time. In other words, once a change is applied, the same test plan is executed and the results are compared with a previous run to see whether the change made had any improved or worsened effect on results. This process repeats till the performance goals of the project have been met.

The performance testing core activities are displayed as follows:

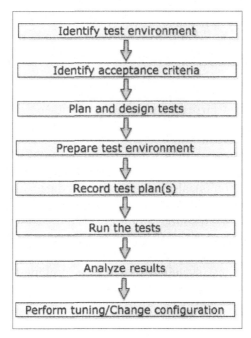

Performance testing core activities

Performance testing is usually a collaborative effort between all parties involved. Parties include business stakeholders, enterprise architects, developers, testers, DBAs, system admins, and network admins. Such collaboration is necessary to effectively gather accurate and valuable results when conducting tests. Monitoring network utilization, database I/O and waits, top queries, and invocation counts helps the team find bottlenecks and areas that need further attention in ongoing tuning efforts.

# Performance testing and tuning

There is a strong relationship between performance testing and tuning, in the sense that one often leads to the other. Often, end-to-end testing unveils system or application bottlenecks that are regarded unacceptable with project target goals. Once those bottlenecks are discovered, the next steps for most teams are a series of tuning efforts to make the application perform adequately.

Such efforts are normally included but are not limited to:

- Configuring changes in system resources
- Optimizing database queries
- Reducing round trips in application calls; sometimes leading to redesigning and re-architecting problematic modules
- Scaling out application and database server capacity
- Reducing application resource footprint
- Optimizing and refactoring code, including eliminating redundancy and reducing execution time

Tuning efforts may also commence if the application has reached acceptable performance but the team wants to reduce the amount of system resources being used, decrease volume of hardware needed, or further increase in system performance.

After each change (or series of changes), the test is re-executed to see whether performance has improved or declined as a result of the changes. The process will be continued with the performance results having reached acceptable goals. The outcome of these test-tuning circles normally produces a baseline.

# Baselines

Baseline is a process of capturing performance metric data for the sole purpose of evaluating the efficacy of successive changes to the system or application. It is important that all characteristics and configurations except those specifically being varied for comparison remain the same in order to make effective comparisons as to which change (or series of changes) is driving results towards the targeted goal. Armed with such baseline results, subsequent changes can be made to the system configuration or application and testing results can be compared to see whether such changes were relevant or not. Some considerations when generating baselines include:

- They are application-specific
- They can be created for system, application, or modules
- They are metrics/results
- They should not be over generalized
- They evolve and may need to be redefined from time to time
- They act as a shared frame of reference
- They are reusable
- They help identify changes in performance

# Load and stress testing

Load testing is the process of putting demand on a system and measuring its response, that is, determining how much volume the system can handle. Stress testing is the process of subjecting the system to unusually high loads far beyond its normal usage pattern to determine its responsiveness. These are different from performance testing whose sole purpose is to determine the response and effectiveness of a system, that is, how fast the system is. Since load ultimately affects how a system responds, performance testing is almost always done in conjunction with stress testing.

# JMeter to the rescue

In the previous section, we covered the fundamentals of conducting a performance test. One of the areas performance testing covers is testing tools. Which testing tool do you use to put the system and application under load? There are numerous testing tools available to perform this operation from free to commercial solutions. However, our focus in this book will be on Apache JMeter, a free open source cross-platform desktop application from The Apache Software foundation. JMeter has been around since 1998 according to historic change logs on its official site, making it a mature, robust, and reliable testing tool. Cost may also have played a role in its wide adoption. Small companies usually may not want to foot the bill for commercial end testing tools, which often place restrictions, for example, on how many concurrent users one can spin off. My first encounter with JMeter was exactly a result of this. I worked in a small shop that had paid for a commercial testing tool, but during the course of testing, we had outrun the licensing limits of how many concurrent users we needed to simulate for realistic test plans. Since JMeter was free, we explored it and were quite delighted with the offerings and the share amount of features we got for free.

Here are some of its features:

- Performance test of different server types including web (HTTP and HTTPS), SOAP, database, LDAP, JMS, mail, and native commands or shell scripts
- Complete portability across various operating systems
- Full multithreading framework allowing concurrent sampling by many threads and simultaneous sampling of different functions by separate thread groups
- **Graphical User Interface (GUI)**
- HTTP proxy recording server
- Caching and offline analysis/replaying of test results
- High extensibility
- Live view of results as testing is being conducted

JMeter allows multiple concurrent users to be simulated on the application allowing you to work towards most of the target goals obtained earlier in this chapter, such as attaining baseline, identifying bottlenecks, and so on.

It will help answer questions such as:

- Will the application still be responsive if 50 users are accessing it concurrently?
- How reliable will it be under a load of 200 users?
- How much of the system resources will be consumed under a load of 250 users?
- What will the throughput look like with 1000 users active in the system?
- What will be the response time for the various components in the application under load?

JMeter, however, should not be confused with a browser (more on this in *Chapter 2, Recording Your First Test* and *Chapter 3, Submitting Forms*). It doesn't perform all the operations supported by browsers, in particular, JMeter does not execute JavaScript found in HTML pages, nor does it render HTML pages the way a browser does. However, it does give you the ability to view request responses as HTML through many of its listeners, but the timings are not included in any samples. Furthermore, there are limitations to how many users can be spun on a single machine. These vary depending on the machine specifications (for example, memory, processor speed, and so on) and the test scenarios being executed. In our experience, we have mostly been able to successfully spin off 250-450 users on a single machine with a 2.2 GHz processor and 8 GB of RAM.

# Up and running with JMeter

Now, let's get up and running with JMeter, beginning with its installation.

## Installation

JMeter comes as a bundled archive so it is super easy to get started with it. Those working in corporate environments behind a firewall or machines with non-admin privileges appreciate this more. To get started, grab the latest binary release by pointing your browser to http://jmeter.apache.org/download_jmeter.cgi. At the time of writing this, the current release version is 2.12. The download site offers the bundle as both .zip file and .tar file. In this book, we go with the .zip file option, but free feel to download the .tgz file if that's your preferred way of grabbing archives.

Once downloaded, extract the archive to a location of your choice. Throughout this book, the location you extracted the archive to will be referred to as JMETER_HOME.

Provided you have a JDK/JRE correctly installed and a JAVA_HOME environment variable set, you are all set and ready to run!

The following screenshot shows a trimmed down directory structure of a vanilla JMeter install:

```
.
├── bin
│   ├── examples
│   │   └── jsp
│   └── templates
├── docs
│   └── resources
├── extras
├── lib
│   ├── ext
│   └── junit
├── licenses
│   ├── bin
│   └── src
└── printable_docs

187 directories
```

JMETER_HOME folder structure

Following are some of the folders in the Apache-JMeter-2.12 as shown in the preceding screenshot:

- bin: This folder contains executable scripts to run and perform other operations in JMeter

- docs: This folder contains a well-documented user guide

- extras: This folder contains miscellaneous items including samples illustrating the usage of the Apache Ant build tool (http://ant.apache.org/) with JMeter and bean shell scripting

- lib: This folder contains utility JAR files needed by JMeter (you may add additional JARs here to use from within JMeter—more on this will be covered later)

- printable_docs: This is the printable documentation

# Installing Java JDK

Follow these steps to install Java JDK:

1. Go to `http://www.oracle.com/technetwork/java/javase/downloads/index.html`.

2. Download Java JDK (not JRE) compatible with the system that you will use to test. At the time of writing, JDK 1.8 (update 20) was the latest and that is what we use throughout this book.

3. Double-click on the executable and follow the on-screen instructions.

>  On Windows systems, the default location for the JDK is under `Program Files`. While there is nothing wrong with this, the issue is that the folder name contains a space, which can sometimes be problematic when attempting to set PATH and run programs such as JMeter depending on the JDK from the command line. With this in mind, it is advisable to change the default location to something such as `C:\tools\jdk`.

# Setting up JAVA_HOME

Here are the steps to set up the `JAVA_HOME` environment variable on Windows and Unix operating systems.

## On Windows

For illustrative purposes, assume that you have installed Java JDK at `C:\tools\jdk`:

1. Go to **Control Panel**.

2. Click on **System**.

3. Click on **Advance System settings**.

4. Add Environment to the following variables:

   ○ **Value**: `JAVA_HOME`
   ○ **Path**: `C:\tools\jdk`

5. Locate **Path** (under system variables, bottom half of the screen).

6. Click on **Edit**.

7. Append `%JAVA_HOME%/bin` to the end of the existing path value (if any).

## On Unix

For illustrative purposes, assume that you have installed Java JDK at /opt/tools/jdk:

1. Open up a terminal window.

2. Export JAVA_HOME=/opt/tools/jdk.

3. Export PATH=$PATH:$JAVA_HOME.

It is advisable to set this in your shell profile settings such as .bash_profile (for bash users) or .zshrc (for zsh users) so you won't have to set it for each new terminal window you open.

## Running JMeter

Once installed, the bin folder under the JMETER_HOME folder contains all the executable scripts that can be run. Based on the operating system that you installed JMeter on, you either execute the shell scripts (.sh file) for operating systems that are Unix/Linux flavored, or their batch (.bat file) counterparts on operating systems that are Windows flavored.

>  JMeter files are saved as XML files with a .jmx extension. We refer to them as test scripts or JMX files in this book.

These scripts include:

- jmeter.sh: This script launches JMeter GUI (the default)

- jmeter-n.sh: This script launches JMeter in non-GUI mode (takes a JMX file as input)

- jmeter-n-r.sh: This script launches JMeter in non-GUI mode remotely

- jmeter-t.sh: This opens a JMX file in the GUI

- jmeter-server.sh: This script starts JMeter in server mode (this will be kicked off on the master node when testing with multiple machines remotely; more on this in Chapter [x])

- mirror-server.sh: This script runs the mirror server for JMeter

- shutdown.sh: This script gracefully shuts down a running non-GUI instance

- stoptest.sh: This script abruptly shuts down a running non-GUI instance

To start JMeter, open a terminal shell, change to the `JMETER_HOME/bin` folder and run the following command on Unix/Linux:

`./jmeter.sh`

Run the following command on Windows:

`jmeter.bat`

A short moment later, you will see the JMeter GUI displayed in the Configuring proxy server section. Take a moment to explore the GUI. Hover over each icon to see a short description of what it does. The Apache JMeter team has done an excellent job with the GUI. Most icons are very similar to what you are used to, which helps ease the learning curve for new adapters. Some of the icons, for example, stop and shutdown, are disabled for now till a scenario/test is being conducted. In the next chapter, we will explore the GUI in more detail as we record our first test script.

On the terminal window, you might see some warnings from Java 8 that some Java options (`PermSize` and `MaxPerSize`) provided will be ignored. Do not be alarmed. JDK 8 came with better memory management and some default Java options used to start JMeter are no longer required, so it ignores them. You can read more about this at the following links:

`http://java.dzone.com/articles/java-8-permgen-metaspace`

`http://www.infoq.com/news/2013/03/java-8-permgen-metaspace`

The environment variable JVM_ARGS can be used to override JVM settings in the `jmeter.bat` or `jmeter.sh` script. Consider the following example:
export JVM_ARGS="-Xms1024m -Xmx1024m -Dpropname=propvalue"

## Command-line options

Running JMeter with incorrect options provides you with usage info. The options provided are as follows:

`./jmeter.sh -`


```
-h, --help
print usage information and exit
-v, --version
print the version information and exit
-p, --propfile<argument>
```

```
thejmeter property file to use
-q, --addprop<argument>
additionalJMeter property file(s)
-t, --testfile<argument>
thejmeter test(.jmx) file to run
-1, --logfile <argument>
the file to log samples to
-j, --jmeterlogfile<argument>
jmeter run log file (jmeter.log)
-n, --nongui
    run JMeter in nongui mode
```

This is a snippet (non-exhaustive list) of what you might see if you did the same. We will explore some, but not all these options as we go through the book.

## JMeter's Classpath

Since JMeter is 100 percent pure Java, it comes packed with functionality to get most of the test cases scripted. However, there might come a time when you need to pull in a functionality provided by a third-party library or one developed by yourself, which is not present by default. As such, JMeter provides two directories where such third-party libraries can be placed to be auto discovered on its classpath:

- `JMETER_HOME/lib`: This is used for utility JARs.
- `JMETER_HOME/lib/ext`: This is used for JMeter components and add-ons. All custom-developed JMeter components should be placed in the `lib/ext` folder, while third-party libraries (JAR files) should reside in the `lib` folder.

## Configuring a proxy server

If you are working from behind a corporate firewall, you may need to configure JMeter to work with it, providing it with the proxy server host and port number. To do so, supply additional command-line parameters to JMeter when starting it up. Some of them are as follows:

- `-H`: This command-line parameter specifies the proxy server hostname or IP address
- `-P`: This specifies the proxy server port
- `-u`: This specifies the proxy server username if it is secure
- `-a`: This specifies the proxy server password if it is secure, for example:
  ```
  ./jmeter.sh -H proxy.server -P 7567 -u username -a password
  ```

On Windows, run the `jmeter.bat` file instead.

> Do not confuse the proxy server mentioned here with JMeter's built-in HTTP Proxy Server, which is used to record HTTP or HTTPS browser sessions. We will be exploring this in the next chapter when we record our first test scenario.

The screen is displayed as follows:

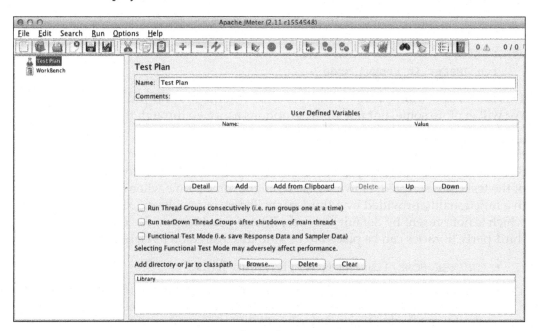

JMeter GUI

## Running in non-GUI mode

As described earlier, JMeter can run in non-GUI mode. This is needed when you run remotely, or want to optimize your testing system by not taking the extra overhead cost of running the GUI. Normally, you will run the default (GUI) when preparing your test scripts and running light load, but run the non-GUI mode for higher loads.

To do so, use the following command-line options:

- `-n`: This command-line option indicates to run in non-GUI mode
- `-t`: This command-line option specifies the name of the JMX test file
- `-l`: This command-line option specifies the name of the JTL file to log results to

- -j: This command-line option specifies the name of the JMeter run log file
- -r: This command-line option runs the test servers specified by the `remote_hosts` JMeter property
- -R: This command-line option runs the test in the specified remote servers (for example, `-Rserver1,server2`)

In addition, you can also use the `-H` and `-P` options to specify proxy server host and post like we saw earlier:

```
./jmeter.sh -n -t test_plan_01.jmx -l log.jtl
```

## Running in server mode

This is used when performing distributed testing, that is, using more testing servers to generate additional load on your system. JMeter will be kicked off in server mode on each remote server (slave) and then a GUI on the master server will be used to control the slave nodes. We will discuss this in detail when we dive into distributed testing in *Chapter 4, Managing Sessions*:

```
./jmeter-server.sh
```

 Specify the `server.exitaftertest=true` JMeter property if you want the server to exit after a single test is completed. It is set as off by default.

## Overriding properties

JMeter provides two ways to override Java, JMeter, and logging properties. One way is to directly edit the `jmeter.properties`, which resides in the JMETER_HOME/bin folder. I suggest that you take a peek into this file and see the vast number of properties you can override. This is one of the things that makes JMeter so powerful and flexible. On most occasions, you will not need to override the defaults, as they have sensible default values.

The other way to override these values is directly from the command line when starting JMeter.

The options available to you include:

- Defining a Java system property value:
  ```
  -D<property name>=<value>
  ```

- Defining a local JMeter property:
  ```
  -J<property name>=<value>
  ```

- Defining a JMeter property to be sent to all remote servers:

  ```
  -G<property name>=<value>
  ```

- Defining a file containing JMeter properties to be sent to all remote servers:

  ```
  -G<property file>
  ```

- Overriding a logging setting, setting a category to a given priority level:

  ```
  -L<category>=<priority>
  ./jmeter.sh -Duser.dir=/home/bobbyflare/jmeter_stuff \
      -Jremote_hosts=127.0.0.1 -Ljmeter.engine=DEBUG
  ```

 Since command-line options are processed after the logging system has been set up, any attempt to use the -J flag to update the log_level or log_file properties will have no effect.

# Tracking errors during test execution

JMeter keeps track of all errors that occur during a test in a log file named jmeter. log by default. The file resides in the folder from which JMeter was launched. The name of this log file, like most things, can be configured in jmeter.properties or via a command-line parameter -j <name_of_log_file>. When running the GUI, the error count is indicated in the top-right corner, that is, to the left of the number of threads running for the test, as shown in Figure 1.4 in the following screenshot. Clicking on it reveals the log file contents directly at the bottom of the GUI. The log file provides an insight into what exactly is going on in JMeter when your tests are being executed and helps determine the cause of error(s) when they occur.

Figure 1.4: JMeter GUI error count/indicator

# Configuring JMeter

Should you need to customize JMeter default values, you can do so by editing the jmeter.properties file in the JMETER_HOME/bin folder, or making a copy of that file, renaming it to something different (for example, my-jmeter.properties), and specifying that as a command-line option when starting JMeter.

Some options you can configure include:

- `xml.parser`: This specifies Custom XML parser implementation. The default value is `org.apache.xerces.parsers.SAXParser`. It is not mandatory. If you found the provided SAX parser buggy for some of your use cases, it provides you with the option to override it with another implementation. For example, you can use `javax.xml.parsers.SAXParser`, provided that the right JARs exist on your instance of JMeter classpath.

- `remote_hosts`: This is a comma-delimited list of remote JMeter hosts (or `host:port` if required). When running JMeter in a distributed environment, list the machines where you have JMeter remote servers running. This will allow you to control those servers from this machine's GUI. This applies only to distributed testing and is not mandatory. More on this will be discussed in *Chapter 6, Distributed Testing*.

- `not_in_menu`: This is a list of components you do not want to see in JMeter's menus. Since JMeter has quite a number of components, you may wish to restrict it to show only components you are interested in or those you use regularly. You may list their classname or their class label (the string that appears in JMeter's UI) here, and they will no longer appear in the menus. The defaults are fine and in our experience, we have never had to customize them, but we list it here so that you are aware of its existence. It is not mandatory.

- `user.properties`: This specifies the name of the file containing additional JMeter properties. These are added after the initial property file, but before the `-q` and `-J` options are processed. This is not mandatory. User properties can be used to provide additional classpath configurations such as plugin paths via the `search_paths` attribute, and utility JAR paths via the `user_classpath` attribute. In addition, these properties files can be used to fine-tune JMeter components' log verbosity.

  - `search_paths`: This specifies a list of paths (separated by `;`) that JMeter will search for JMeter add-on classes; for example additional samplers. This is in addition to any of the JARs found in the `lib/ext` folder. This is not mandatory. This comes in handy, for example, when extending JMeter with additional plugins that you don't intend to install in the `JMETER_HOME/lib/ext` folder. You can use this to specify an alternate location on the machine to pick up the plugins. Refer to *Chapter 4, Managing Sessions*.

  - `user.classpath`: In addition to JARs in the `lib` folder, use this attribute to provide additional paths that JMeter will search for utility classes. It is not mandatory.

- `system.properties`: This specifies the name of the file containing additional system properties for JMeter to use. These are added before the -S and -D options are processed. This is not mandatory. This typically provides you with the ability to fine-tune various SSL settings, key stores, and certificates.

    ° `ssl.provider`: This specifies the custom SSL implementation if you don't want to use the built-in Java implementation. This is not mandatory. If, for some reason, the default built-in Java implementation of SSL, which is quite robust, doesn't meet your particular usage scenario, this allows you to provide a custom one. In our experience, the default has always been sufficient.

The command-line options are processed in the following order:

- `-p profile`: This specifies the custom jmeter properties file to be used. If present, it is loaded and processed. This is optional.

- `jmeter.properties` file: This is the default configuration file for JMeter and is already populated with sensible default values. It is loaded and processed after any user-provided custom properties file.

- `-j logfile`: This is optional. It specifies the jmeter logfile. It is loaded and processed after the jmeter.properties file that we discussed previously.

- Logging is initialized.

- `user.properties`: is loaded (if any).

- `system.properties`: is loaded (if any).

- All other command-line options are processed.

# Summary

In this chapter, we have covered the fundamentals of performance testing. We also discussed key concepts and activities surrounding performance testing in general. In addition, we installed JMeter and you learned how to get it fully running on a machine and explored some of the configurations available with it. We explored some of the options that make JMeter a great tool of choice for your next performance testing assignment. These include the fact it is free and mature, open sourced, easily extensible and customizable, completely portable across various operating systems, is a great plugin eco-system, has a large user community, built-in GUI and recording, and validating test scenarios among others. In comparison with the other tools for performance testing, JMeter holds its stance.

In the next chapter, we will record our first test scenario and dive deeper into JMeter.

# 2
# Recording Your First Test

JMeter comes with a built-in test script recorder, also referred to as a proxy server (http://en.wikipedia.org/wiki/Proxy_server), to aid you in recording test plans. The test script recorder, once configured, watches your actions as you perform operations on a website, creates test sample objects for them, and eventually stores them in your test plan, which is a JMX file. In addition, JMeter gives you the option to create test plans manually, but this is mostly impractical for recording nontrivial testing scenarios. You will save a whole lot of time using the proxy recorder, as you will be seeing in a bit.

So without further ado, let's record our first test! For this, we will record the browsing of JMeter's own official website as a user will normally do. For the proxy server to be able to watch your actions, it will need to be configured. This entails two steps:

1. Setting up the HTTP(S) Test Script Recorder within JMeter.
2. Setting the browser to use the proxy.

## Configuring the JMeter HTTP(S) Test Script Recorder

The first step is to configure the proxy server in JMeter. To do this, we perform the following steps:

1. Start JMeter.
2. Add a thread group, as follows:
3. Right-click on **Test Plan** and navigate to **Add | Threads (User) | Thread Group**.

4. Add the HTTP(S) Test Script Recorder element, as follows:

5. Right-click on **WorkBench** and navigate to **Add** | **Non-Test Elements** | **HTTP(S) Test Script Recorder.**

6. Change the port to 7000 **(1)** (under **Global Settings**).

7. You can use a different port, if you choose to. What is important is to choose a port that is not currently used by an existing process on the machine. The default is 8080.

8. Under the **Test plan content** section, choose the option **Test Plan > Thread Group (2)** from the **Target Controller** drop-down.

9. This allows the recorded actions to be targeted to the thread group we created in step 2.

10. Under the **Test plan content** section, choose the option **Put each group in a new transaction controller (3)** from the **Grouping** drop-down.

11. This allows you to group a series of requests constituting a page load. We will see more on this topic later.

12. Click on **Add suggested Excludes** (under **URL Patterns to Exclude**).

13. This instructs the proxy server to bypass recording requests of a series of elements that are not relevant to test execution. These include JavaScript files, stylesheets, and images. Thankfully, JMeter provides a handy button that excludes the often excluded elements.

14. Click on the **Start** button at the bottom of the **HTTP(S) Test Script Recorder** component.

15. Accept the **Root CA certificate** by clicking on the **OK** button.

With these settings, the proxy server will start on port 7000, and monitor all requests going through that port and record them to a test plan using the default recording controller. For details, refer to the following screenshot:

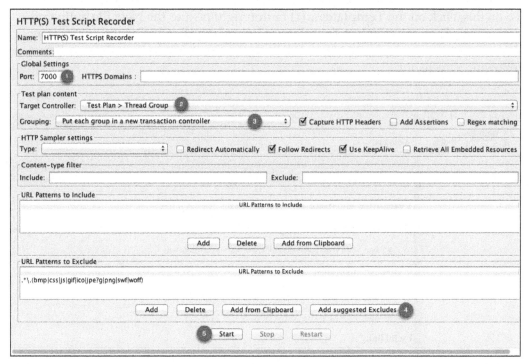

Configuring the JMeter HTTP(S) Test Script Recorder

 In older versions of JMeter (before version 2.10), the now HTTP(S) Test Script Recorder was referred to as HTTP Proxy Server.

While we have configured the HTTP(S) Test Script Recorder manually, the newer versions of JMeter (version 2.10 and later) come with prebundled templates that make commonly performed tasks, such as this, a lot easier. Using the bundled recorder template, we can set up the script recorder with just a few button clicks. To do this, click on the **Templates…(1)** button right next to the New file button on the toolbar. Then select **Select Template** as **Recording (2)**. Change the port to your desired port (for example, **7000**) and click on the **Create (3)** button. Refer to the following screenshot:

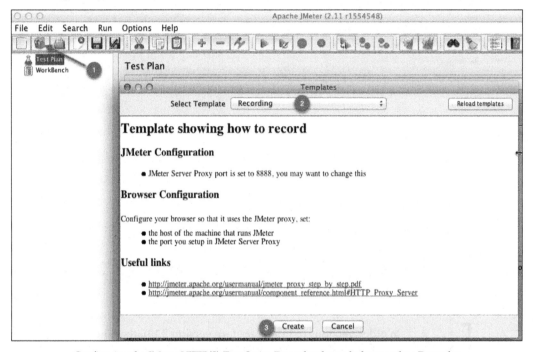

Configuring the JMeter HTTP(S) Test Script Recorder through the template Recorder

# Setting up your browser to use the proxy server

There are several ways to set up the browser of your choice to use the proxy server. We'll go over two of the most common ways, starting with my personal favorite, which is using a browser extension.

# Using a browser extension

Google Chrome and Firefox have vibrant browser plugin ecosystems that allow you to extend the capabilities of your browser with each plugin that you choose. For setting up a proxy, I really like **FoxyProxy** (http://getfoxyproxy.org/). It is a neat add-on to the browser that allows you to set up various proxy settings and toggle between them on the fly without having to mess around with setting systems on the machine. It really makes the work hassle free. Thankfully, FoxyProxy has a plugin for Internet Explorer, Chrome, and Firefox. If you are using any of these, you are lucky! Go ahead and grab it!

# Changing the machine system settings

For those who would rather configure the proxy natively on their operating system, we have provided the following steps for Windows and Mac OS.

On Windows OS, perform the following steps for configuring a proxy:

1. Click on **Start**, then click on **Control Panel**.
2. Click on **Network and Internet**.
3. Click on **Internet Options**.
4. In the **Internet Options** dialog box, click on the **Connections** tab.
5. Click on the **Local Area Network (LAN) Settings** button.
6. To enable the use of a proxy server, select the checkbox for **Use a proxy server for your LAN (These settings will not apply to dial-up or VPN connections)**, as shown in the following screenshot.
7. In the proxy **Address** box, enter localhost in the IP address.
8. In the **Port** number text box, enter 7000 (to match the port you set up for your JMeter proxy earlier).
9. If you want to bypass the proxy server for local IP addresses, select the **Bypass proxy server for local addresses** checkbox.

10. Click on **OK** to complete the proxy configuration process.

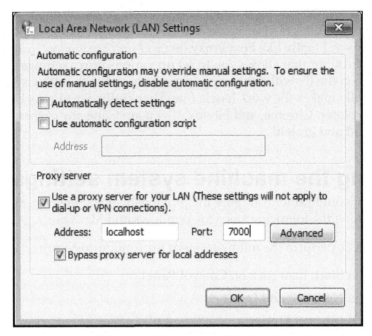

Manually setting proxy on Windows 7

On Mac OS, perform the following steps to configure a proxy:

1. Go to **System Preference**.
2. Click on **Network**.
3. Click on the **Advanced...** button.
4. Go to the **Proxies** tab.
5. Select the **Web Proxy (HTTP)** checkbox.
6. Under **Web Proxy Server**, enter localhost.
7. For port, enter 7000 (to match the port you set up for your JMeter proxy earlier).
8. Do the same for **Secure Web Proxy (HTTPS)**.

9. Click on **OK**.

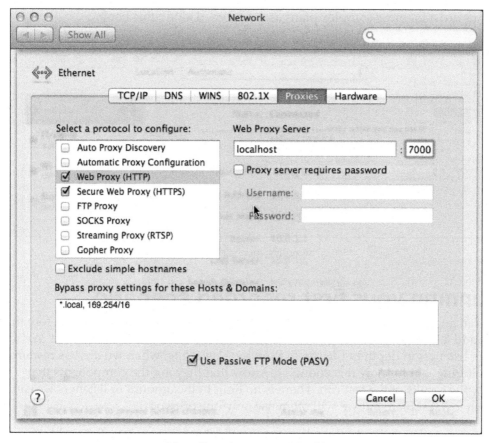

Manually setting proxy on Mac OS

For all other systems, please consult the related operating system documentation.

Now that is all out of the way and the connections have been made, let's get to recording using the following steps:

1. Point your browser to `http://jmeter.apache.org/`.
2. Click on the **Changes** link under **About**.
3. Click on the **User Manual** link under **Documentation**.
4. Stop the HTTP(S) Test Script Recorder by clicking on the **Stop** button, so that it doesn't record any more activities.
5. If you have done everything correctly, your actions will be recorded under the test plan. Refer to the following screenshot for details.

Congratulations! You have just recorded your first test plan. Admittedly, we have just scrapped the surface of recording test plans, but we are off to a good start. We will record a lot more complex plans as we proceed along this book.

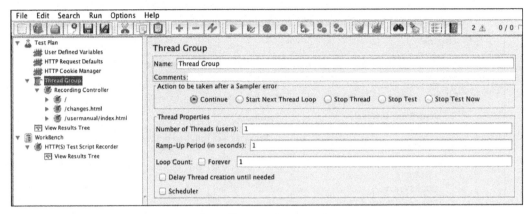

Recording your first scenario

# Running your first recorded scenario

We can go right ahead and replay or run our recorded scenario now, but before that let's add a listener or two to give us feedback on the results of the execution. We will cover listeners in depth in *Chapter 5, Resource Monitoring*, when we discuss resource monitoring, but for now it is enough to know that they are the components that show the results of the test run. There is no limit to the amount of listeners we can attach to a test plan, but we will often use only one or two.

For our test plan, let's add three listeners for illustrative purposes. Let's add a Graph Results listener, a View Results Tree listener, and an Aggregate Report listener. Each listener gathers a different kind of metric that can help analyze performance test results as follows:

1. Right-click on **Test Plan** and navigate to **Add | Listener | View Results Tree**.

2. Right-click on **Test Plan** and navigate to **Add | Listener | Aggregate Report**.

3. Right-click on **Test Plan** and navigate to **Add | Listener | Graph Results**.

Just as we can see more interesting data, let's change some settings at the thread group level, as follows:

1. Click on **Thread Group**.

2. Under **Thread Properties** set the values as follows:
   - ° **Number of Threads (users)**: 10
   - ° **Ramp-Up Period (in seconds)**: 15
   - ° **Loop Count**: 30

This will set our test plan up to run for ten users, with all users starting their test within 15 seconds, and have each user perform the recorded scenario 30 times. Before we can proceed with test execution, save the test plan by clicking on the save icon.

Once saved, click on the start icon (the green play icon on the menu) and watch the test run. As the test runs, you can click on the **Graph Results** listener (or any of the other two) and watch results gathering in real time. This is one of the many features of JMeter.

From the Aggregate Report listener, we can deduce that there were 600 requests made to both the changes link and user manual links, respectively. Also, we can see that most users (**90% Line**) got very good responses below 200 milliseconds for both. In addition, we see what the throughput is per second for the various links and see that there were no errors during our test run.

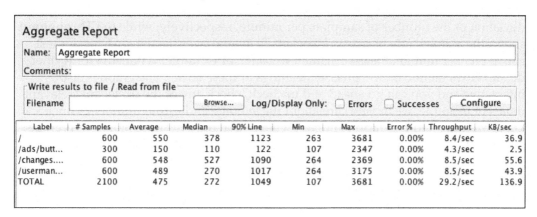

| Label | # Samples | Average | Median | 90% Line | Min | Max | Error % | Throughput | KB/sec |
|---|---|---|---|---|---|---|---|---|---|
| / | 600 | 550 | 378 | 1123 | 263 | 3681 | 0.00% | 8.4/sec | 36.9 |
| /ads/butt... | 300 | 150 | 110 | 122 | 107 | 2347 | 0.00% | 4.3/sec | 2.5 |
| /changes.... | 600 | 548 | 527 | 1090 | 264 | 2369 | 0.00% | 8.5/sec | 55.6 |
| /userman... | 600 | 489 | 270 | 1017 | 264 | 3175 | 0.00% | 8.5/sec | 43.9 |
| TOTAL | 2100 | 475 | 272 | 1049 | 107 | 3681 | 0.00% | 29.2/sec | 136.9 |

Results as seen through this Aggregate Report listener

Looking at the View Results Tree listener, we can see exactly the changes link requests that failed and the reasons for their failure. This can be valuable information to developers or system engineers in diagnosing the root cause of the errors.

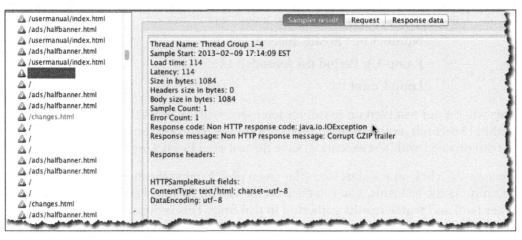

Results as seen via the View Results Tree Listener

The Graph Results listener also gives a pictorial representation of what is seen in the View Tree listener in the preceding screenshot. If you click on it as the test goes on, you will see the graph get drawn in real time as the requests come in. The graph is a bit self-explanatory with lines representing the average, median, deviation, and throughput. The **Average**, **Median**, and **Deviation** all show average, median, and deviation of the number of samplers per minute, respectively, while the **Throughput** shows the average rate of network packets delivered over the network for our test run in bits per minute. Please consult a website, for example, Wikipedia for further detailed explanation on the precise meanings of these terms. The graph is also interactive and you can go ahead and uncheck/check any of the irrelevant/relevant data. For example, we mostly care about the average and throughput. Let's uncheck **Data**, **Median**, and **Deviation** and you will see that only the data plots for **Average** and **Throughput** remain. Refer to the following screenshot for details.

With our little recorded scenario, you saw some major components that constitute a JMeter test plan. Let's record another scenario, this time using another application that will allow us to enter form values. We will explore this more in the next chapter, but for now let's have a sneak peek.

# Excilys Bank case study

We'll borrow a website created by the wonderful folks at Excilys, a company focused on delivering skills and services in IT (http://www.excilys.com/). It's a light banking web application created for illustrative purposes. Let's start a new test plan, set up the test script recorder like we did previously, and start recording.

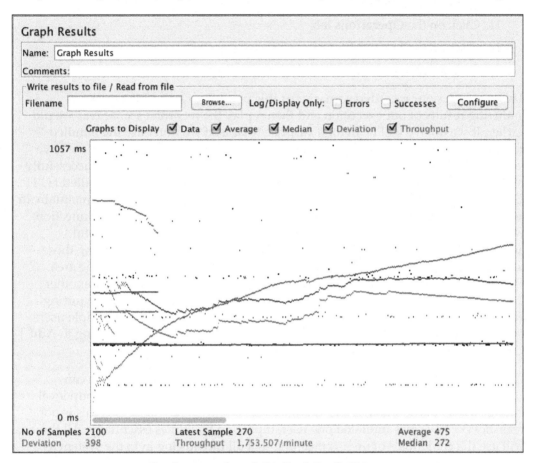

Results as seen through this Graph Results Listener

Let's start with the following steps:

1.  Point your browser to http://excilysbank.aws.af.cm/public/login.html.

2.  Enter the username and password in the login form, as follows:

3.  **Username**: user1

4.  **Password**: password1

5.  Click on the **PERSONNAL CHECKING** link.

6.  Click on the **Transfers** tab.

7.  Click on **My Accounts**.

8.  Click on the **Joint Checking** link.

9.  Click on the **Transfers** tab.

10. Click on the **Cards** tab.

11. Click on the **Operations** tab.

12. Click on the **Log out** button.

13. Stop the proxy server by clicking on the **Stop** button.

This concludes our recorded scenario. At this point, we can add listeners for gathering results of our execution and then replay the recorded scenario as we did earlier. If we do, we will be in for a surprise (that is, if we don't use the bundled recorder template). We will have several failed requests after login, since we have not included the component to manage sessions and cookies needed to successfully replay this scenario. Thankfully, JMeter has such a component and it is called HTTP Cookie Manager. This seemingly simple, yet powerful component helps maintain an active session through HTTP cookies, once our client has established a connection with the server after login. It ensures that a cookie is stored upon successful authentication and passed around for subsequent requests, hence allowing those to go through. Each JMeter thread (that is, user) has its own cookie storage area. That is vital since you won't want a user gaining access to the site under another user's identity. This becomes more apparent when we test for websites requiring authentication and authorization (like the one we just recorded) for multiple users. Let's add this to our test plan by right-clicking on **Test Plan** and navigating to **Add | Config Element | HTTP Cookie Manager**.

Once added, we can now successfully run our test plan. At this point, we can simulate more load by increasing the number of threads at the thread group level. Let's go ahead and do that. If executed, the test plan will now pass, but this is not realistic. We have just emulated one user, repeating five times essentially. All threads will use the credentials of user1, meaning that all threads log in to the system as user1. That is not what we want. To make the test realistic, what we want is each thread authenticating as a different user of the application. In reality, your bank creates a unique user for you, and only you or your spouse will be privileged to see your account details. Your neighbor down the street, if he used the same bank, won't get access to your account (at least we hope not!). So with that in mind, let's tweak the test to accommodate such a scenario.

# Parameterizing the script

We begin by adding a CSV Data Set Config component (**Test Plan | Add | Config Element | CSV Data Set Config**) to our test plan. Since it is expensive to generate unique random values at runtime due to high CPU and memory consumption, it is advisable to define that upfront. The CSV Data Set Config component is used to read lines from a file and split them into variables that can then be used to feed input into the test plan. JMeter gives you a choice for the placement of this component within the test plan. You would normally add the component at the HTTP request level of the request that needs values fed from it. In our case, this will be the login HTTP request, where the username and password are entered. Another is to add it at the thread group level, that is, as a direct child of the thread group. If a particular dataset is applied to only a thread group, it makes sense to add it at this level. The third place where this component can be placed is at the Test Plan root level. If a dataset applies to all running threads, then it makes sense to add it at the root level. In our opinion, this also makes your test plans more readable and maintainable, as it is easier to see what is going on when inspecting or troubleshooting a test plan since this component can easily be seen at the root level rather than being deeply nested at other levels. So for our scenario, let's add this at the Test Plan root level.

 You can always move the components around using drag and drop even after adding them to the test plan.

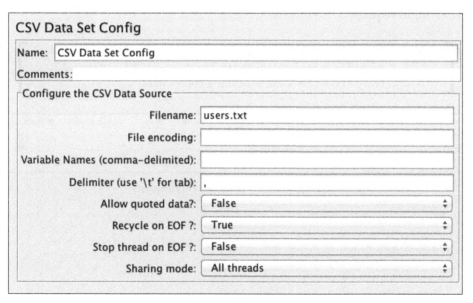

CSV Data Set Config

Once added, the **Filename** entry is all that is needed if you have included headers in the input file. For example, if the input file is defined as follows:

```
user, password, account_id
user1, password1, 1
```

If the **Variable Names** field is left blank, then JMeter will use the first line of the input file as the variable names for the parameters. In cases where headers are not included, the variable names can be entered here. The other interesting setting here is **Sharing mode**. By default, this defaults to **All threads**, meaning all running threads will use the same set of data. So in cases where you have two threads running, Thread1 will use the first line as input data, while Thread2 will use the second line. If the number of running threads exceeds the input data then entries will be reused from the top of the file, provided that **Recycle on EOF** is set to **True** (the default). The other options for sharing modes include **Current thread group** and **Current thread**. Use the former for cases where the dataset is specific for a certain thread group and the latter for cases where the dataset is specific to each thread. The other properties of the component are self-explanatory and additional information can be found in JMeter's online user guide.

Now that the component is added, we need to parameterize the login HTTP request with the variable names defined in our file (or the csvconfig component) so that the values can be dynamically bound during test execution. We do this by changing the value of the username to ${user} and password to ${password}, respectively, on the HTTP login request.

 The values between the ${ } match the headers defined in the input file or the values specified in the Variable Names entry of the CSV Data Set Config component.

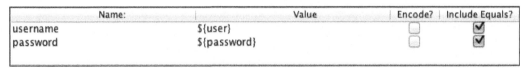

| Name: | Value | Encode? | Include Equals? |
|---|---|---|---|
| username | ${user} | ☐ | ☑ |
| password | ${password} | ☐ | ☑ |

Binding parameter values for HTTP requests

We can now run our test plan and it should work as earlier, only this time the values are dynamically bound through the configuration we have set up. So far, we have run for a single user. Let's increase the thread group properties and run for ten users, with a ramp-up of 30 seconds, for one iteration. Now let's rerun our test. Examining the test results, we notice some requests failed with a status code of **403** (`http://en.wikipedia.org/wiki/HTTP_403`), which is an access denied error. This is because we are trying to access an account that does not seem to be the logged-in user. In our sample, all users made a request for account number 4, which only one user (`user1`) is allowed to see. You can trace this by adding a View Tree listener to the test plan and returning the test.

If you closely examine some of the HTTP requests in the Request tab of the View Results Tree listener, you'll notice requests as follows:

```
/private/bank/account/ACC1/operations.html
/private/bank/account/ACC1/year/2013/month/1/page/0/operations.json
...
```

Observant readers would have noticed that our input data file also contains an `account_id` column. We can leverage this column so that we can parameterize all requests containing account numbers to pick the right accounts for each logged-in user. To do this, consider the following line of code:

```
/private/bank/account/ACC1/operations.html
```

Change this to the following line of code:

```
/private/bank/account/ACC${account_id}/operations.html
```

Now, consider the following line of code:

```
/private/bank/account/ACC1/year/2013/month/1/page/0/operations.json
```

Change this to the following line of code:

```
/private/bank/account/ACC${account_id}/year/2013/month/1/page/0/
operations.json
```

Make similar changes to the rest of the code. Go ahead and do this for all such requests. Once completed, we can now rerun our test plan and, this time, things are logically correct and will work fine. You can also verify that if all works as expected after the test execution by examining the View Results Tree listener, clicking on some account requests URL, and changing the response display from text to HTML, you should see an account other than `ACCT1`.

# Extracting information during test run

This brings us to one more scenario to explore. Sometimes, it is useful to parse the response to get the required information rather than sending it as a column of the input data. The parsed response can be any textual format. These include JSON, HTML, TXT, XML, CSS, and so on. This can further help to make your test plans more robust. In our preceding test plan, we could have leveraged this feature and parsed the response to get the required account number for users, rather than sending it along as input parameters. Once parsed and obtained, we can then save and use the account number for other requests down the chain. Let's go ahead and record a new test plan as we did before. Save it under a new name. To aid us in extracting a variable from the response data, we will use one of JMeter's postprocessor components, Regular Expression Extractor. This component runs after each sample request in its scope, applying the regular expression and extracting the requested values. A template string is then generated and the result of this is stored into a variable name. This variable name is then used to parameterize, such as in the case of CSV Data Set Config we saw earlier.

We'll add a Regular Expression Extractor component as a child element of the HTTP request to `/private/bank/accounts.html` just below the `/login` request. Unlike the CSV Data Set Config component we saw earlier, this component has to be placed directly as a child element of the request on which it will act, hence a Post-Processor component. Its configuration should be as shown in the following screenshot:

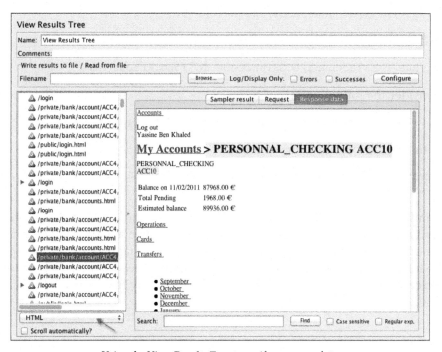

Using the View Results Tree to verify response data

When configuring the Regular Expression Extractor component, use the following values for each of the indicated fields:

- **Apply to**: **Main sample only**
- **Response Field to check**: **Body**
- **Reference Name**: `account_id`
- **Regular Expression**: `<td class="number">ACC(\d+)</td>`
- **Template**: `$1$`
- **Match No.(0 for Random)**: `1`
- **Default Value**: `NOT_FOUND`

The following screenshot shows what the component will look like with all the entries filled out:

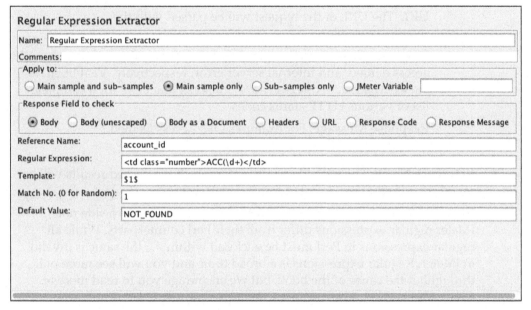

Configuring the Regular Expression Extractor

Once configured, proceed to parameterize the other requests for accounts with the `${account_id}` variable like we did earlier. At this point, we are able to rerun our test plan and get exactly the similar behavior and output as we did before we fed in a dataset, which also had `account_id` as a column. You have now seen two ways to get the same information when building your own test plans. Though your use case will mostly vary from those we have examined here, the same principles will be applied.

Here is a brief summary of the various configuration variables for the Regular Expression Extractor component:

- **Apply to**: The default **Main sample only** is almost always okay, but there are times when the sample contains child samples that request for embedded resources. The options allow you to target either the main sample, subsamples, or both. The last option is that the JMeter variable allows assertions to be applied to the contents of the named variable.

- **Response field to check**: This parameter specifies which field the regular expression should apply to. The options include:

    ○ **Body**: This is the body of the response, excluding headers.

    ○ **Body (unescaped)**: This is the body of the response with all HTML escape codes replaced.

    ○ **Headers**: These may not be present for non-HTTP samples.

    ○ **URL**: The URL of the request will be parsed with the regular expression.

    ○ **Response Code**: For example, 200, 403, 500 meaning success, access denied, and internal server error, respectively. Visit `http://en.wikipedia.org/wiki/HTTP_200#2xx_Success` for a complete list of various HTTP status codes.

    ○ **Response Message**: For example, OK, Access Denied, Internal server error.

- **Reference Name**: The variable name under which the parsed results will be saved. This is what will be used for parameterization.

- **Regular Expression**: Enter any valid regular expression. As a side note, JMeter regular expressions differ from their Perl counterparts. While all regular expressions in Perl must be enclosed within `//`, the same is invalid in JMeter. Regular expressions is a broad topic and you will see more of it throughout the cause of the book, but we encourage you to read more at `http://en.wikipedia.org/wiki/Regular_expression`.

- **Template**: This is the template used to create a string from the matches found. This is an arbitrary string with special elements to refer to a group such as `$1$` to refer to `group 1`, `$2$` to refer to `group 2`, and so on. `$0$` refers to whatever the expression matches. In our example, `$0$` would refer to `ACC<td class="number">ACC4</td>`, for example, and `$1$` refers to `ACC4`.

- **Match No. (0 for Random)**: This parameter indicates which match to use since the regular expression may match multiple times:

    - `0`: This indicates that JMeter should be used to match at random.

    - `N`: A positive number `N` means to select the *nth* match.

    - `refName`: The value of the template.

    - `refName_gn`: Where `n` is the groups for the match, for example, 1,2,3, and so on.

    - `refName_g`: The number of groups in the regular expression (excluding `0`).

[   Note that when no matches occur, `refName_g0`, `refName_g1`, and `refName_g` variables are all removed and the `refName` value is set to the default value, if present. ]

    - Negative numbers can be used in conjunction with a ForEach controller.

    - `refName_matchNr`: This is the number of matches found. It could be 0.

    - `refName_n`: Where `n` is the number of strings as generated by the template, for example, 1, 2, 3, and so on.

    - `refName_n_gm`: Where `m` is the number of groups for the match, for example, 0, 1, 2, and so on.

    - `refName`: This is set to the default value (if present).

    - `refName_gn`: This is not set.

**Default Value**: If the regular expression doesn't match, then the variable will be set to the default value set. This is an optional parameter, but I recommend that you always set it as it helps to debug and diagnose issues while creating your test plans.

# Anatomy of a JMeter test

With the samples we have explored so far, we have seen a similar pattern emerging. We have seen what mostly constitutes a JMeter test plan. We'll use the remainder of this chapter to explore the anatomy and composition of the JMeter tests.

# Test plan

This is the root element of the JMeter scripts and houses the other components such as Threads, Config Elements, Timers, PreProcessors, PostProcessors, Assertions, and Listeners. It also offers a few configurations of its own.

First off, it allows you to define user variables (name-value pairs) that can be used later in your scripts. It also allows the configuration of how the thread groups that it contains should run, that is, should thread groups run one at a time? As test plans evolve over time, you'll often have several thread groups contained within a test plan. This option allows you determine how they run. By default, all thread groups are set to run concurrently. A useful option when getting started is the Functional Test Mode. When checked, all the server responses returned from each sample are captured. This can prove useful for small simulation runs ensuring that JMeter is configured correctly and the server is returning the expected results, but the downside is that JMeter will see performance degradation and file sizes can be huge. It is off by default and shouldn't be checked when conducting real test simulations. One more useful configuration is the ability to add third-party libraries that can be used to provide additional functionality for test cases. The time will come when your simulation needs additional libraries that are not bundled with JMeter by default. At such times, you can add those JARs through this configuration.

# Thread groups

Thread groups, like we have seen, are the entry points of any test plan. They represent the number of threads/users JMeter will use to execute the test plan. All controllers and samplers for a test must reside under a thread group. Other elements, such as listeners, may be placed directly under a test plan in cases where you want them to apply to all the thread groups, or under a thread group, if they only pertain to that group. Thread group configurations provide options to specify the number of threads that will be used for the test plan, how long it will take for all threads to become active (ramp-up), and the number of times the test will be executed. Each thread will execute the test plan completely independently of other threads. JMeter spins off multiple threads to simulate concurrent connections to the server. It is important that the "ramp-up" be long enough to avoid too large a workload at the start of a test as this can often lead to network saturation and invalidate test results. If the intention is to have x number of users active in the system, it is better to ramp-up slowly and increase the number of iterations. A final option the configuration provides is the scheduler. This allows setting the starting and ending time of a test execution. For example, you can kick-off a test to run during off-peak hours for exactly one hour.

# Controllers

Controllers drive the processing of a test and come in two flavors: sampler controllers and logic controllers.

Sampler controllers send requests to a server. These include HTTP, FTP, JDBC, LDAP, and so on. Although JMeter has a comprehensive list of samplers, we will mostly focus on HTTP request samplers in this book, since we are focusing on testing web applications.

Logical controllers, on the other hand, allow the customization of the logic used to send the requests. For example, a loop controller can be used to repeat an operation a certain number of times. The if controller is for selectively executing a request, and the while controller for continuing to execute a request till some condition becomes false, and so on. At the time of writing, JMeter 2.12 comes bundled with 16 different controllers, each serving different purposes.

# Samplers

These components help send requests to the server and wait for a response. Requests are processed in the order they appear in the tree. JMeter comes bundled with the following samplers:

- HTTP request
- JDBC request
- LDAP request
- SOAP/XML-RPC request
- Webservice (SOAP) request
- FTP request

Each of these has properties that can further be tweaked to suit your needs. In most cases, the default configurations are fine and can be used as it is. Consider adding assertions to samplers to perform basic validation on server responses. Often during testing, the server may return a status code 200, indicative of a successful request, but might fail to display the page correctly. At such times, assertions can help to ensure that the request was indeed successful as indicated.

# Logic controllers

These help customize the logic used to decide how requests are sent to a server. They can modify requests, repeat requests, interleave requests, control the duration of requests' execution, switch requests, measure the overall time taken to perform requests, and so on. At the time of writing, JMeter comes bundled with total of 16 logic controllers. Please visit the online user guide (`http://jmeter.apache. org/usermanual/component_reference.html#logic_controllers`) to see a comprehensive list and details on each.

# Test fragments

A special type of controller is used purely for code reuse within a test plan. They exist on the test plan tree at the same level as the thread group element and are not executed unless referenced either by an Include or Module Controller.

# Listeners

These components gather the results of a test run, allowing it to be further analyzed. In addition, listeners provide the ability to direct the data to a file for later use. Furthermore, it allows to define which fields are saved and whether to use CSV or XML format. All listeners save the same data with the only difference being the way the data is presented on screen. Listeners can be added anywhere in the test, including directly under the test plan. They will collect data only from the elements at or below their level.

JMeter comes bundled with about 18 different listeners all serving different purposes. Though you will often only use a handful of them, it is advisable to become familiar with what each offers to know when to use them.

> Some listeners such as Assertion Results, Comparison Assertion Visualizer, Distribution Graph, Graph Results, Spline Visualizer, and View Results in tree are memory and CPU intensive and should not be used during actual test runs. They are okay to be used for debugging and functional testing.

# Timers

By default, JMeter threads send requests without pausing between each request. It is recommended that you specify a delay by adding one of the available timers to thread groups. This also helps make your test plans more realistic as real users couldn't possibly send requests at that pace. The timer causes JMeter to pause a certain amount of time before each sampler that is in its scope.

# Assertions

Assertion components allow you to verify responses received from the server. In essence, they allow you to verify that the application is functioning correctly and that the server is returning the expected results. Assertions can be run on XML, JSON, HTTP, and other forms of responses returned from the server. Assertions can also be resource intensive, so ensure that you don't have them on for actual test runs.

# Configuration elements

Configuration elements work closely with a sampler, enabling requests to be modified or added to. They are only accessible from inside the tree branch where you place the element. These elements include HTTP Cookie Manager, HTTP Header Manager, and so on.

# Preprocessor and postprocessor elements

A preprocessor element, like the name implies, executes some actions prior to a request being made. Preprocessor elements are often used to modify the settings of a request just before it runs or to update variables that aren't extracted from the response text.

Postprocessor elements execute some actions after a request has been made. They are often used to process response data and extract value from it.

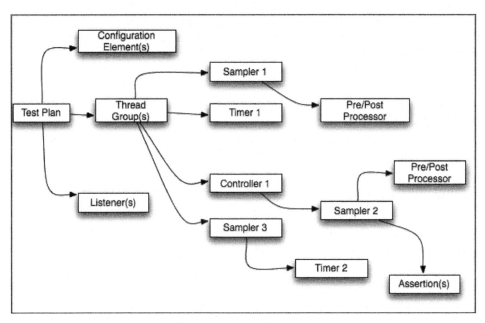

The anatomy of a JMeter test

# Summary

We have covered quite a lot in this chapter. You learned how to configure JMeter and our browsers to help record test plans. In addition, you learned about some built-in components that can help us feed data into our test plan and/or extract data from server responses. In addition, you learned what composes a JMeter test plan and got a good grasp on those components.

In the next chapter, we will dive deeper into form submission and explore more JMeter components.

# 3
# Submitting Forms

In this chapter, we'll expand on the foundations we started building on in *Chapter 2, Recording Your First Test*, and we will dive deeper into the details of submitting forms. While most of the forms you encounter while recording test plans might be simple in nature, some are a completely different beast and require careful attention. For example, more and more websites are embracing RESTful web services, and as such, you would mainly interact with JSON objects when recording or executing test plans for such applications. Another area of interest will be recording applications that make heavy use of AJAX to accomplish business functionality. Google, for one, is known to be a mastermind at this. Most of their products, including Search, Gmail, Maps, YouTube, and so on, all use AJAX extensively. Occasionally, you might have to deal with XML response data, for example, extracting parts of it to use for samples further down the chain in your test plan. You might also come across cases when you need to upload a file to the server or download one from it.

For all these and more, we will explore some practical examples in this chapter and gain some helpful insights as to how to deal with these scenarios when you come across them as you prepare your test plans.

## Capturing simple forms

We have already encountered a variation of form submission in *Chapter 2, Recording Your First Test*, when we submitted a login form to be authenticated with the server. The form had two text fields for username and password, respectively. This is a good start. Most websites requiring authentication will have a similar feel to them. HTML forms, however, span a whole range of other input types. These include checkboxes, radio buttons, select and multiselect drop-down lists, text area, file uploads, and so on. In this section, we take a look at handling other HTML input types.

We have created a sample application that we will use throughout most of this chapter to illustrate some of the concepts that we will discuss. The application can be reached by visiting `http://jmeterbook.aws.af.cm`. Take a minute to browse around and take it for a manual spin so as to have an idea what the test scripts we record will be doing.

# Handling checkboxes

Capturing checkbox submission is similar to capturing textboxes, which we encountered earlier in *Chapter 2, Recording Your First Test*. Depending on the use case, there might be one or more related/unrelated checkboxes on a form. Let's run through a scenario for illustrative purposes. With your JMeter proxy server running and capturing your actions, perform the following steps:

1. Go to `http://jmeterbook.aws.af.cm/form1/create`.
2. Enter a name in the textbox.
3. Check a hobby or two.
4. Click on the **submit** button.

At this point, if you examine the recorded test plan, the `/form1/submit` post request has the following parameters:

- **Name**: This represents the value entered in the textbox
- **Hobbies**: You can have one or more depending on the number of hobbies you checked off
- **submit**: This is the value of the **submit** button

We can then build upon the test plan by adding a CSV Data Set Config component to the mix to allow us to feed different values for the names and hobbies (refer to *handling-chechboxes.jmx* at `https://github.com/ptwj/ptwj-code/blob/master/chap3/handling-checkboxes.jmx` ). Finally, we can expand the test plan further by parsing the response from the `/form1/create` sample to determine what hobbies are available on the form using a Post-Processor element (for example, Regular Expression Extractor) and then randomly choosing one or more of them to be submitted. We'll leave that as an exercise for you. Handling multiselect is no different from this.

# Handling radio buttons

Radio buttons are normally used as option fields on a web page, that is, they are normally grouped together to present a series of choices to the user allowing them to select one per each group. Things such as marital status, favorite food, polls, and so on are practical uses of these buttons. Capturing their submission is quite similar to dealing with checkboxes, just that we will only have one entry per submission for each radio group. Our sample at `http://jmeterbook.aws.af.cm/radioForm/` `index` has only one radio group, allowing users to identify their marital status. Hence after recording this, we will only have one entry submission for a user.

Let's follow the given steps:

1. Go to `http://jmeterbook.aws.af.cm/radioForm/index`.
2. Enter a name in the textbox.
3. Enter your marital status.
4. Click on the **submit** button.

Viewing the HTML source of the page (right-click anywhere on the page and select **View Page Source**) would normally get you the "IDs" that the server expects to be returned for each option presented on the page. Armed with this information, we can expand our input test data allowing us to run the same scenario for more users with varying data. As always, you can use a Post-Processor component to further eliminate the need to send the radio button IDs to your input feed. Handling a drop-down list is no different from this scenario. Handling all other forms of HTML input types for example text, text area, and so on falls under the categories we have explored so far.

# Handling file uploads

You may encounter situations where uploading a file to the server is part of the functionality of the system under test. JMeter can also help in this regard. It comes with a built-in multipart/form-data option on post requests, which is needed by HTML to correctly process file uploads. In addition to checking the option to make a post request multipart, you will need to specify the absolute path of the file, in cases where the file you are uploading is not within JMeter's bin directory, or the relative path in cases where the file resides within JMeter's bin directory. Let's record a scenario illustrating this:

1. Go to `http://jmeterbook.aws.af.cm/uploadForm`.
2. Enter name in the textbox.
3. Choose a file to upload by clicking on the **Choose File** button.
4. Click on **Submit**.

Note that for our test application, files uploaded can't be larger than 1 MB.

Depending on the location of the file you choose, you might encounter an error similar to this:

```
java.io.FileNotFoundException: Argentina.png (No such file or directory)
    at java.io.FileInputStream.open(Native Method)
    at java.io.FileInputStream.<init>(FileInputStream.java:120)
    at org.apache.http.entity.mime.content.FileBody.writeTo(FileBody.java:92)
    at org.apache.jmeter.protocol.http.sampler.HTTPHC4Impl$ViewableFileBody.writeTo(HTTPHC4Impl.java:773)
```

Do not be alarmed! This is because JMeter is expecting to find the file in its `bin` directory. You will have to either tweak the file location in the recorded script to point the absolute path of the file or place it in the `bin` directory or a subdirectory thereof. For the sample packaged with this book, we have opted to place the files in a subdirectory under the `bin` directory (`$JMETER_HOME/bin/samples/images`). Examine the file `handling-file-uploads.jmx`.

# Handling file downloads

Another common situation you may encounter will be testing a system that has file download capabilities exposed as a function to its users. Users, for example, might download reports, user manuals, documentation, and so on from a website. Knowing how much strain this can put on the server can be an area of interest to stakeholders. JMeter provides the ability to record and test such scenarios. As an example, let's record a user retrieving a PDF tutorial from JMeter's website.

Let's follow the given steps:

1. Go to `http://jmeterbook.aws.af.cm/`.
2. Click on the **Handling File Downloads** link.
3. Click on the **Access Log Tutorial** link.

This should stream a PDF file to your browser. You can add a View Tree Listener and examine the response output after playing back the recording. You can also add a Save Responses to file `Listener` and have JMeter save the contents of the response to a file that you can later inspect. This is the route we have opted for in the sample recorded with this book. Files will be created in the `bin` directory of the JMeter's installation directory. Refer to *handling-file-downloads-1.jmx* (`https://github.com/ptwj/ptwj-code/blob/master/chap3/handling-file-downloads-1.jmx`). Also, using Save Responses to file `Listener` is useful for cases where you want to capture the response, in this case, a file, and feed it to other actions further in the test scenario. For example, we could have saved the response and used it to upload the file to another section of the same server, or to a different server entirely.

# Posting JSON data

**REST (Representational State Transfer)** is a simple stateless architecture that generally runs over HTTP/HTTPS. Requests and responses are built around the transfer of representations of resources. It emphasizes interactions between clients and services by providing a limited number of operations (GET, POST, PUT, and DELETE). The GET method fetches the current state of a resource, the POST method creates a new resource, the PUT method updates an existing resource, and the DELETE method destroys the resource. Flexibility is provided by assigning resources their own unique **Universal Resource Indicators (URIs)**. Since each operation has a specific meaning, REST avoids ambiguity. In modern times, the typical object structure passed between a client and server is JSON. More information about REST can be found at `http://en.wikipedia.org/wiki/REST`.

When dealing with websites that expose RESTful services in one form or the other, you will most likely have to interact with JSON data in some way. Such websites may provide means to create, update, and delete data on the server via posting JSON data. URLs can also be provided to return existing data in JSON format. This happens even more in the most modern websites, which use AJAX to an extent, as we use JSON when interacting with AJAX. In all such scenarios, you will need to be able to capture and post data to the server using JMeter. JSON, also known as JavaScript Object Notation, is a text-based open standard designed for human readable data interchange. You can find more information about it at `http://en.wikipedia.org/wiki/JSON` and `http://www.json.org/`. For this book, it will suffice to know what the structure of a JSON object looks like. Consider the following example:

```
{"empNo": 109987, "name": "John Marko", "salary": 65000}
```

Also, consider this example:

```
[{
  "id":1,
  "dob":"09-01-1965",
  "firstName":"Barry",
  "lastName":"White",
"jobs":[{"id":1,"description":"Doctor"}, {"id":2,"description":"Firem
an"}]
}]
```

Some basic rules of thumb when dealing with JSON are as follows:

- [] – indicates a list of objects
- {} – indicates an object definition
- "key": "value" – define string values of an object, under a desired key
- "key": value – define integer values of an object, under a desired key

The example that we just saw shows an employee object with employee number 109987, whose name is John Marko, and earns $65,000. The second sample shows a person named Barry White, born on 9/1/1965 who is both a doctor and fireman.

Now that we covered a sample JSON structure, let's examine how JMeter can help with posting JSON data. The example website provides a URL to save the Person object. A person has a first name, a last name, and a date of birth attribute. In addition, a person can hold multiple jobs. A valid JSON structure to store a person may look like the following code:

```
{"firstName":"Malcom", "lastName":"Middle", "dob": "2/2/1965",
"jobs":[{"id": 1, "id": 2}]}
{"firstName":"Sarah", "lastName":"Martz", "dob": "3/7/1971"}
```

Instead of recording, we will manually construct the test scenario for this case since we have intentionally not provided a form to save a person's entry so as to give you hands-on experience with writing test plans for such scenarios.

Let's post JSON data by following these steps:

1. Launch **JMeter**.
2. Add a thread group to the test plan (right-click on **Test Plan** and navigate to **Add | Threads (Users) | Thread Group**).
3. Add an HTTP Request Sampler component to the thread group (right-click on **Thread Group** and navigate to **Add | Sampler | HTTP Request**).
4. Under **HTTP Request**, change implementation to **HttpClient4**.
5. Fill the properties of the HTTP Request Sampler component, as follows:
   - **Server Name or IP**: jmeterbook.aws.af.cm
   - **Method**: POST
   - **Path**: /person/save
6. Click on the **Body Data** tab to fill in the JSON data to fill in the following code as:

```
{
  "firstName": "Bob",
  "lastName": "Jones",
  "jobs": [
    {
      "id": "3"
    }
  ]
}
```

7. Add an HTTP Header Manager component to the HTTP Request Sampler component (right-click on **HTTP Request Sampler** and navigate to **Add | Config Element | HTTP Header Manager**).
8. Add a View Results Tree Listener to the thread group (right-click on **Thread Group** and navigate to **Add | Listener | View Results Tree**).
9. Save the test plan.

If you have done all this correctly, your HTTP Request Sampler component will look like the following screenshot:

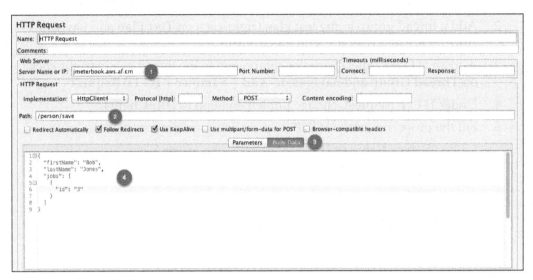

Configuring HTTP Request Sampler to post JSON

Now you will be able to run the test, and if all was correctly set, Bob Jones will now be saved on the server. You can verify that by examining View Results Tree Listener. The request should be green and in the **Response data** tab, you should see Bob Jones listed as one of the entries. Even better yet, you can view the last 10 stored entries in the browser directly at http://jmeterbook.aws.af.cm/person/list.

Of course all other tricks you learned so far apply here as well. We can use a CSV Data Config element to parameterize the test and have variation in our data input. Refer to *posting-json.jmx* for this. Regarding input data variation, since jobs are optional for this input set, it may make sense to parameterize the whole JSON string read from the input feed to give you more variation.

For example, you can replace the value with ${json} and let the input CSV Data have entries such as:

```
json
{"firstName":"Malcom", "lastName":"Middle", "dob": "1/2/1971",
"jobs":[{"id": 1, "id": 2}]}
{"firstName":"Sarah", "lastName":"Martz", "dob": "6/9/1982"}
```

It is important to put each record on a separate line. We'll leave that as an exercise for you. Although simplistic in nature, what we covered here will give you all the information you need to post JSON data when recording your test plans.

When dealing with RESTful requests in general, it helps to have some tools handy to examine requests, inspect responses, and view network latency, among many others. The following is a list of handy tools that can help:

- **Firebug** (Firefox, Chrome and IE browser add-on): `http://getfirebug.com/`
- **Chrome developer tools**: `https://developers.google.com/chrome-developer-tools/`
- **Advance REST Client** (chrome browser extension): `http://bit.ly/15BEKlV`
- **REST Client** (Firefox browser add-on): `http://mzl.la/h8YMlz`

# Reading JSON data

Now that we know how to post JSON data, let's take a brief look at how to consume them in JMeter. Depending on the use case, you may find yourself dealing more with reading JSON than posting them. JMeter provides a number of ways to digest this information, store them if needed, and use them further down the chain in your test plans. Let's start with a simple use case. The example website has a link that provides usage of the last 10 entries of persons stored on the server. It can be reached by visiting `http://jmeterbook.aws.af.cm/person/list`.

If we were to process the JSON response and use the first and last name further down the chain, we can use a Regular Expression Extractor PostProcessor to extract these. Let's create a test plan to do just that.

Let's follow the given steps:

1. Launch **JMeter**.
2. Add a thread group to the test plan (right-click on **Test Plan** and navigate to **Add | Threads (Users) | Thread Group**).
3. Add a HTTP Request Sampler to the thread group (right-click on **Thread Group** and navigate to **Add | Sampler | HTTP Request**).
4. Under **HTTP Request**, change implementation to `HttpClient4`.
5. Fill the properties of the HTTP Request Sampler, as follows:
    - **Server Name or IP**: `jmeterbook.aws.af.cm`
    - **Method**: `GET`
    - **Path**: `/person/list`

6. Add a Regular Expression Extractor as a child of the HTTP Request Sampler (right-click on **HTTP Request Sampler** and navigate to **Add | Post Processors | Regular Expression Extractor**):

   ◦ **Reference Name**: name

   ◦ **Regular Expression**: `"firstName":"(\w+?)",.+?,"lastName":"(\w+?)"`

   ◦ **Template**: `$1$$2$`

   ◦ **Match No**: 1

   ◦ **Default Value**: name

7. Add Debug Sampler to the thread group (right-click on **Thread Group** and navigate to **Add | Sampler | Debug Sampler**).

8. Add a View Results Tree Listener to the thread group (right-click on **Thread Group** and navigate to **Add | Listener | View Results Tree**).

9. Save the test plan.

The interesting bit is the cryptic regular expression that we use here. It describes the words to be matched and stores them in variables defined as name. The \w+? instructs the pattern engine not to be greedy when matching and to stop on the first occurrence. The full capabilities of regular expressions are beyond the scope of this book, but I encourage you to master it some as it will help you while scripting your scenarios. For now, just believe that it does what it says. Once you execute the test plan, you will be able to see the matches in the debug sampler of the View Results Tree. Here's a snippet of what you should expect to see:

```
name=firstName0lastName0
name_g=2
name_g0="firstName":"Larry","jobs":[{"id":1,"description":"Doctor"}],"
lastName":"Ellison"
name_g1=Larry
name_g2=Ellison
server=jmeterbook.aws.af.cm
```

Now, let's shift gears to a more complicated example.

# Using BSF PostProcessor

When dealing with more complicated JSON structures, you might find that the Regular Expression Extractor PostProcessor doesn't remove it. You might struggle to come up with the right regular expression to extract all the info you need. Examples of that might be deeply nested object graphs that have embedded lists of objects in them. At such times, a **BSF PostProcessor** will fit the bill. **Bean Scripting Framework (BSF)** is a set of Java classes that provides scripting language support within Java applications. This opens a whole realm of possibilities allowing you to leverage the knowledge and power of scripting languages within your test plan, while still retaining access to Java class libraries. Scripting languages supported within JMeter at the time of writing include Groovy, JavaScript, BeanShell, Jython, Perl, and Java to name a few. Let's jump right in with an example querying Google's search service.

Let's follow the given steps:

1. Launch **JMeter**.
2. Add a thread group to the test plan (right-click on **Test Plan** and navigate to **Add | Threads (Users) | Thread Group**).
3. Add a HTTP Request Sampler to the thread group (right-click on **Thread Group** and navigate to **Add | Sampler | HTTP Request**).
4. Under **HTTP Request**, change implementation to `HttpClient4`.
5. Fill the properties of the HTTP Request Sampler as follows:
   - **Server Name or IP**: `ajax.googleapis.com`
   - **Method**: `GET`
   - **Path**: `/ajax/services/search/web?v=1.0&q=jmeter`
6. Add a BSF PostProcessor as a child of the HTTP Request Sampler (right-click on **HTTP Request Sampler** and navigate to **Add | Post Processors | BSF PostProcessor**):
   - Pick `JavaScript` in the language drop-down list
   - In the scripts text area, enter this:
     ```
     // Turn the JSON into an object called 'response'
     eval('var response = ' + prev.getResponseDataAsString());

     vars.put("url_cnt", response.responseData.results.length);

     //for each result, stop the URL as a JMeter variable
     ```

```
for (var i = 0; i <= response.responseData.results.length;
i++)
{
    var x = response.responseData.results[i];
  vars.put("url_" + i, x.url);
}
```

7. Add a Debug Sampler to the thread group (right-click on **Thread Group** and navigate to **Add | Sampler | Debug Sampler**).

8. Add a View Results Tree Listener to the thread group (right-click on **Thread Group** and navigate to **Add | Listener | View Results Tree**).

9. Save the test plan.

Once saved, you can execute the test plan and see the full JSON returned by the request and the extracted values that have now been stored as JMeter variables. If all is correct, you will see values similar to these:

```
url_0=http://jmeter.apache.org/
url_1=http://jmeter.apache.org/download_jmeter.cgi
url_2=http://jmeter.apache.org/usermanual/
url_3=http://en.wikipedia.org/wiki/Apache_JMeter
url_cnt=4
```

The BSF PostProcessor exposes a few variables that can be used in your scripts by default. In our preceding example, we have used two of them (prev and var). The prev variable gives access to the previous sample's result and the var variable gives read/write access to variables. Refer to a list of available variables at http://jmeter. apache.org/usermanual/component_reference.html#BSF_PostProcessor.

Consider the following code:

```
eval('var response = ' + prev.getResponseDataAsString());
```

A quick rundown of the code retrieves the response data of the previous sampler as string and uses the JavaScript eval() function to turn it into a JSON structure. Take a look at the JavaDocs at http://jmeter.apache.org/api/org/apache/jmeter/ samplers/SampleResult.html to see all other methods available for the prev variable. Once a JSON structure has been extracted, we can call methods like we would normally do in JavaScript:

```
vars.put("url_cnt", response.responseData.results.length);
```

This gets the size of how many results were returned and stores the results in a JMeter variable url_cnt. The final bit of code iterates through the results and extracts the actual URLs and stores them into distinct JMeter variables url_0 through url_3.

The same can be achieved with any of the other supported scripting languages. An equivalent script in Groovy will be as follows:

```
import groovy.json.*

// Turn the JSON into an object called 'response'
def response = prev.responseDataAsString
def json = new JsonSlurper().parseText(response)

vars.put("url_cnt", json.responseData.results.size as String)

for (int i = 0; i < json.responseData.results.size; i++)
{
    def result = json.responseData.results.get(i)
    vars.put("url_" + i, result.url)
}
```

For this to work, however, you will need to download the `groovy-all-2.3.x.jar` file and put it in your `$JMETER_HOME/lib` directory. In addition, you will have to ensure that groovy is selected as the scripting language in the BSF PostProcessor component.

# Handling XML responses

Yet another structure you may encounter as you build test plans is XML. Some websites may hand off XML as their response to certain calls. **XML (Extensible Markup Language)** allows you to describe object graphs in a different format than JSON does. For example, we can get our test application to return an XML representation of the list of persons we were working with earlier in this chapter by making a call to `http://jmeterbook.aws.af.cm/person/list?format=xml`. Describing XML in detail goes beyond the scope of this book, but you can find much more about it online. For our exercise, it suffices just to know what they look like. Take a look at the XML returned by the previous link. Now that you know what XMLs look like, let's get going with a sample test plan that deals with retrieving an XML response and extracting variables from it. Take a look at the XML that we will parse at `http://search.maven.org/remotecontent?filepath=org/springframework/spring-test/3.2.1.RELEASE/spring-test-3.2.1.RELEASE.pom`. Our goal is to extract all the `artifactId` elements (deeply nested within the structure) into variables that we can use later in our test plan, if we choose.

Let's follow the given steps:

1. Launch **JMeter**.

2. Add a thread group to the test plan (right-click on **Test Plan** and navigate to **Add | Threads (Users) | Thread Group**).

3. Add a HTTP Request Sampler to the thread group (right-click on **Thread Group** and navigate to **Add | Sampler | HTTP Request**).

4. Under **HTTP Request**, change implementation to `HttpClient4`.

5. Fill the properties of the `HTTP Request Sampler` as follows:

   ○ **Server Name or IP**: `search.maven.org`

   ○ **Method**: `GET`

   ○ **Path**: `/remotecontent?filepath=org/springframework/spring-test/3.2.1.RELEASE/spring-test-3.2.1.RELEASE.pom`

6. Add a `Save Responses` to a file `Listener` as a child of the `HTTP Request Sampler` (right-click on **HTTP Request Sampler** and navigate to **Add | Listener | Save Responses to a file**) with the following properties:

   ○ **Filename prefix**: `xmlSample_`

   ○ **Variable name**: `testFile`

7. Add a XPath Extractor as a child of the HTTP Request Sampler (right-click on **HTTP Request Sampler** and navigate to **Add | Post Processors | XPath Extractor**): with the following properties:

   ○ **Reference name**: `artifact_id`

   ○ **XPath query**: `project/dependencies/dependency/artifactId`

   ○ **Default value**: `artifact_id`

8. Add a Debug Sampler to the thread group (right-click on **Thread Group** and navigate to **Add | Sampler | Debug Sampler**).

9. Add a View Results Tree Listener to the thread group (right-click **Thread Group** and navigate to **Add | Listener | View Results Tree**).

10. Save the test plan.

Once saved, you will be able to execute the test plan and see the `artifact_id` variables in the View Tree Listener. The only new element we used here is the XPath Extractor Post-Processor. This nifty JMeter component allows you to use XPath query language to extract values from a structured XML or (X)HTML response. As such, we can extract an element deeply nested in the structure with this simple query `project/dependencies/dependency/artifactId`.

This will look for the tail element (`artifactId`) of the query string within the structure, as follows:

```
<project...>
  ...
  <dependencies>
    <dependency>
      <groupId>javax.activation</groupId>
      <artifactId>activation</artifactId>
      <version>1.1</version>
      <scope>provided</scope>
    </dependency>
    ...
  </dependencies>
</project>
```

This will return `activation`, for example. This is exactly the information we are interested in. Now you know just how to get at the information you need when dealing with XML responses.

# Summary

In this chapter, we went through the details of how to capture form submission in JMeter. We covered simple forms with checkboxes and radio buttons. The same concepts covered in those sections can be equally applied to other input form elements such as text areas, combo boxes, and so on. We further explored how to deal with file uploads and downloads when recording test plans. Along the way, we addressed working with JSON data, both posting and consuming them. This exposed us to two powerful and flexible JMeter Post-Processors, Regular Expression Extractor, and BSF PostProcessor. Finally, we took a look at how to deal with XML data when we encounter them. For that, we covered yet another Post-Processors that JMeter offers, XPath Extractor PostProcessor. You will now be able to use what you learned so far to accomplish most tasks you need to with forms while planning and scripting your test plans.

In the next chapter, we will dive into managing sessions with JMeter and see how we can leverage some of the components provided by JMeter to handle web application HTTP sessions.

# 4
# Managing Sessions

In this chapter, we'll cover session management in JMeter in detail. Web applications, by their very nature, use client and server sessions; both work in harmony to give each user a distinct enclosure to maintain a series of communications with the server without affecting other users. For example, in *Chapter 2, Recording Your First Test*, the server session was created the moment a user logged in to the application, and was maintained for all requests sent to the server by that user until he/she logged off or timed out. This is what protects other users from seeing each other's information. Depending on the application's architecture, the session may be maintained through cookies (most commonly used) or URL rewriting (less commonly used). The former maintains the session by sending a cookie in the HTTP headers of each request, while the latter rewrites the URLs to append the session ID. The main difference is that the former relies on a client's browser choosing to accept cookies and is transparent to the application developer, while the latter isn't transparent and works regardless of whether cookies are enabled or not. That being said, diving into the details of the two modes goes beyond the scope of this book, but I'll encourage you to spend some time reading some online resources to gain better understanding if you are the curious type. For this book, it will suffice to know that there are two modes and that JMeter handles both.

Let's dig right in and explore these scenarios and see how JMeter deals with each.

# Managing sessions with cookies

A majority of web applications rely on cookies to maintain the session state. In the very early stages of the Internet, cookies were only used to keep the session ID. Things have evolved since then and cookies now store a lot more information, such as user IDs and location preferences. The banking application we used as a case study in *Chapter 2, Recording Your First Test*, for example, relies on cookies to help each user maintain a valid session with the server, enabling the user to make a series of requests to the server. An example will help clear things up, so let's get right to one. For our example, some resources are protected based on the role of the user that is logged in. Users can have an admin or user role. The steps to manage sessions with cookies are as follows:

1. Launch JMeter.
2. Start the Test Script Recorder (refer to *Chapter 2, Recording Your First Test*, if you don't know how).
3. In the browser, go to `http://jmeterbook.aws.af.cm/`.
4. Click on the **User Protected Resource** link (under **Chapter 4**).
5. Log in.
6. Enter `user1` in the **Username** field.
7. Enter `password` in the **Password** field.
8. Click on **Link** under **User resources**.
9. Log out.
10. Save the test plan.

Attempting to execute the recorded scenario on saving it will not yield the expected results. Go ahead and add a **View Results Tree** listener (right-click on **Test Plan** and go to **Add | Listener | View Results Tree**) to diagnose what is actually going on. Once the simulation is run, examine the responses from the server through the **View Results Tree** listener. Even though all responses are green, indicating successful requests (since we got a response code of 200 from the server), we are actually still just getting back the login page after successfully logging in (see the **Response** tab of **View Results Tree** for subsequent requests after successful authentication). Ensure that you switch to the HTML view from the drop-down menu to correctly have the page rendered to see things more clearly.

If you examine the **Request** tab, then you will see the reason for using that. Here is a snippet of the Request data of the login process. You will see something similar to this:

```
GET
   http://jmeterbook.aws.af.cm/;jsessionid=2CE58BC032344AA90CA60C6C880
687A4


[no cookies]

Request Headers:
Connection: keep-alive
Content-Type: application/x-www-form-urlencoded
Accept-Language: en-US,en;q=0.8
Accept:
   text/html,application/xhtml+xml,application/xml;q=0.9,*/*;q=0.8
Origin: http://jmeterbook.aws.af.cm
User-Agent: Mozilla/5.0 (Macintosh; Intel Mac OS X 10_8_2)
   AppleWebKit/537.22 (KHTML, like Gecko) Chrome/25.0.1364.99
      Safari/537.22
Accept-Charset: ISO-8859-1,utf-8;q=0.7,*;q=0.3
Cache-Control: max-age=0
Referer: http://jmeterbook.aws.af.cm/login/auth
Accept-Encoding: gzip,deflate,sdch
Host: jmeterbook.aws.af.cm
```

You will notice two things here. First, there is a [no cookies] line present, indicating JMeter didn't find any stored cookie to use for this request. Second is the jsessionid cookie in the first line of the request. The server uses this to group all requests from a user under the same session ID, once authentication is established. If you compare this with the subsequent calls in **View Results Tree**, you will notice different jsessionid values, further indicating that the server is treating those subsequent calls as new requests and not associating it with a previous request. Third, the URL for subsequent calls also mimics what we saw earlier in http:// jmeterbook.aws.af.cm/login/auth, indicating that we are actually being asked to authenticate again on the login page since the server didn't associate our requests for protected resources with the same jsessionid cookie.

The following snippet is displayed as:

```
GET
   http://jmeterbook.aws.af.cm/login/auth;jsessionid=0B478A8A1F93D68D14
745261D0A7E792

[no cookies]
...
```

All this is evidence that JMeter is not currently managing the session appropriately, but how can it? We have not instructed it to. JMeter comes with a couple of components to help maintain sessions. Since our sample here relies on cookies to maintain sessions, we will use the **HTTP Cookie Manager** component. This component stores and sends cookies just as web browsers do. If an HTTP request and response contains a cookie, the Cookie Manager automatically stores that cookie and will use it for all future requests to the application.

> Since a thread is synonymous to a user in JMeter, each thread has its own cookie storage area, giving us the ability to run multiple users for a simulation with each maintaining a separate session.

This is exactly what we want. Let's go ahead and add a Cookie Manager to our test plan. Right-click on **Test Plan** and navigate to **Test Plan | Add | Config Element | HTTP Cookie Manager** (refer to following screenshot). This component allows you to define additional cookies, but the default will usually suffice except in cases where your application might be doing something tricky. Once this is added, if we rerun our test plan and examine the **Request** tab, we will see a different outcome. This time, the jsessionid cookie is stored and maintained across requests and the [no cookie] line is gone. Here is a snippet of the two subsequent requests in **View Results Tree**:

```
GET http://jmeterbook.aws.af.cm/login/auth

Cookie Data:
JSESSIONID=013FA93C2AABB31EBE8FDF8CCC575F09
GET http://jmeterbook.aws.af.cm/secure/user

Cookie Data:
JSESSIONID=013FA93C2AABB31EBE8FDF8CCC575F09
```

Note that the same session ID is maintained across the requests. If you examine the Response data, you will see that you are now able to access the intended protected resources. Refer to the following screenshot, which shows how to use the **HTTP Cookie Manager** component to define additional cookies:

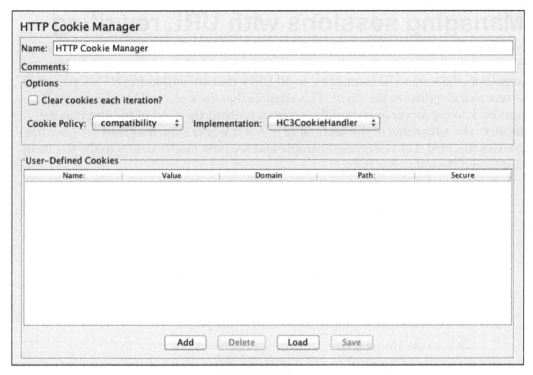

HTTP Cookie Manager

This completes our exploration of the **HTTP Cookie Manager** element. It is possible to have more than one Cookie Manager in a test plan depending on the application needs. For example, if you have multiple thread groups within a test plan, it is possible to have a Cookie Manager per thread group.

> If there are more than one Cookie Managers in the scope of a sampler, there is no way to specify which will be used. Also, a cookie stored in one Cookie Manager is not available to any other manager, so exercise caution when using multiple Cookie Managers.

# Managing sessions with URL rewriting

In the absence of cookie support, the alternative method web applications use to manage session information is a technique known as **URL rewriting**. With this approach, the session ID is attached to all URLs that are within the HTML page that is sent as a response to the client. This ensures that the session ID is automatically sent back to the server as part of the request, without the need of putting it in the header. The advantage of this technique is that it works even if a client browser has cookies disabled. Let's examine a sample and see how JMeter comes to the rescue by displaying the following steps:

1. Launch JMeter.
2. Start the HTTP proxy server (refer to *Chapter 2, Recording Your First Test*, if you don't know how).
3. In the browser, go to `http://jmeterbook.aws.af.cm`.
4. Click on the **URL Rewrite Sample link** under **Chapter 4**.
5. Click on **First Link**.
6. Click on **Another Link** (at the bottom of the page).
7. Click on the **Home** link.
8. Click on **Second Link**.
9. Click on the **jmeter-book** link on the banner on the navigation bar at the top.
10. Save the test plan.

If you re-execute the test plan after saving it, you'll notice that all the links have a `jsessionid` cookie appended to them. This ensures that the same session ID is sent along to the server, thereby treating our series of requests as one whole conversation with the server; in short, our session is maintained. Since we recorded this, the session ID sent with all the requested links is the one that the server generated at the time we recorded. Obviously, we will need to turn this into a variable that can then be used for multiple threads, as each new thread will be treated as a new user with each getting their own unique session ID.

To do this, we'll employ JMeter's **HTTP URL Re-writing Modifier** component. This component is similar to the **HTML Link Parser** modifier except that its specific purpose is to extract session IDs from the response, that is, a page or link. Let's add this to the test plan (right-click on **Thread Group** and navigate to **Thread Group | Pre Processors | HTTP URL Re-writing Modifier**). Refer to the following screenshot to see what the configuration elements are. The most important parameter is **Session Argument Name**. This allows you to specify the session ID parameter name to grab from the response. This may vary based on your application. Java web applications, for example, usually have this as `jsessionid` (as in our case) or `JSESSIONID`. Web applications that are not written in Java might have a variation of this, for example, `SESSION_ID`. Inspect the application under test and note the key that the session ID is getting stored on. This value is what goes into this parameter box. In our case, it is simply `jsessionid`. Refer to the following screenshot to see the configuration elements of **HTTP URL Re-writing Modifier**:

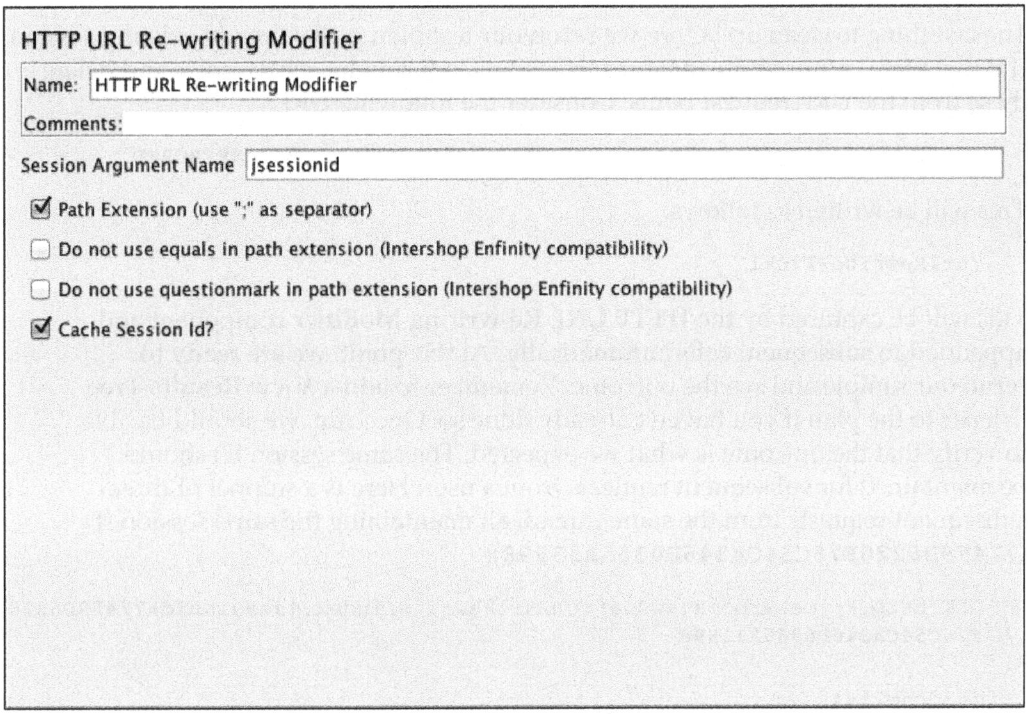

HTTP URL Re-writing Modifier

The other options that can be configured are:

- **Path Extension**: If checked, a semicolon will be used to separate the session ID and the argument URL. Java web applications fall into this category, so go ahead and check it for our sample.

- **Do not use equals in path extension**: If checked, this omits the use of = when capturing the rewrite URL. However, Java web applications use =, so we leave this unchecked.

- **Do not use questionmark in path extension**: This prevents the query string from ending up in the path extension. We will leave it unchecked.

- **Cache Session Id**: This saves the value of the session ID for later use, when it is not present, for example, in subsequent page requests. We check this option as it applies to us. We want the same session ID sent for all page requests by a thread/user.

The last thing to clean up before we rerun our test plan is the already existing session IDs that were captured during our recording. Go through each sampler and delete these from the URL request paths. Consider the following URL:

```
/urlRewrite/link1;jsessionid=9074385741E66F07B36286763FF8C2FD
```

This will be written as follows:

```
/urlRewrite/link1
```

This will be captured by the **HTTP URL Re-writing Modifier** component and appended to subsequent calls automatically. At this point, we are ready to rerun our sample and see the outcome. Remember to add a **View Results Tree** listener to the plan if you haven't already done so. Once run, we should be able to verify that the outcome is what we expected. The same session ID should be maintained for subsequent requests from a user. Here is a snippet of three subsequent requests from the same thread, all maintaining the same session ID (**774F9D6220F76C54CA346D0365A33998**):

```
GET http://jmeterbook.aws.af.cm/urlRewrite/index;jsessionid=774F9D6220
F76C54CA346D0365A33998

[no cookies]

Request Headers:
Connection: keep-alive
Accept-Language: en-US,en;q=0.5
Accept: text/html,application/xhtml+xml,application/
xml;q=0.9,*/*;q=0.8
```

```
User-Agent: Mozilla/5.0 (Macintosh; Intel Mac OS X 10.8; rv:16.0)
  Gecko/20100101 Firefox/16.0
Referer: http://jmeterbook.aws.af.cm/
Accept-Encoding: gzip, deflate
Host: jmeterbook.aws.af.cm

GET http://jmeterbook.aws.af.cm/urlRewrite/link1;jsessionid=774F9D6220
F76C54CA346D0365A33998

GET http://jmeterbook.aws.af.cm/urlRewrite/link3;jsessionid=774F9D6220
F76C54CA346D0365A33998
```

Although we have placed the element at the `Thread Group` level, it can be placed at the sampler level. In such a case, it will only modify that request and not affect subsequent calls. You may need such flexibility in some situations.

This wraps up the different ways in which we can manage sessions with JMeter. The web applications you test will normally fall under these two major categories, cookie management and URL rewriting. Based on your needs, JMeter provides components to help manage sessions for both.

# Summary

In this chapter, we covered how JMeter helps manage web sessions for your test plans. First, we examined the most common way in which web applications manage sessions — using a cookie. For these cases, JMeter provides a component called **HTTP Cookie Manager**, whose primary job is to help capture the cookie generated by the server and store it for future use during test execution. We then explored web applications that use URL rewriting to maintain sessions as opposed to cookies. This led us to **HTTP URL Re-writing Modifier**, another component that JMeter provides for handling these cases.

In conclusion, what we have covered here should suffice in helping you effectively manage sessions as you build test plans for your own applications.

In the next chapter, we will cover resource monitoring.

# 5
# Resource Monitoring

So far, we have seen how JMeter can help with conducting performance testing. In this chapter, we will explore what it offers in terms of resource monitoring. Resource monitoring is a broad subject that covers analyzing system hardware usage, which includes CPU, memory, disk, and network. As you conduct testing, it is important to know how each of these resources behave under load to better understand when there are bottlenecks and address them accordingly. Most organizations have dedicated teams (for example, network and system engineers) to configure and monitor these resources. In addition, there are dedicated tools to monitor and analyze them. Tools such as HP OpenView, CA Wily Introscope (now CA Application Performance Management), New Relic, profiler agent probes, and so on were created for this sole purpose. I said all this to say that what JMeter offers pales in comparison to what you will get using such dedicated tools. Notwithstanding this, not all companies can afford such tools, or have personnel in charge of setting up adequate monitoring. You may just be a one-man shop doing testing and monitoring all by yourself!

Since this is a book on JMeter, let's see how we can go about doing some resource monitoring with it.

# Basic server monitoring

JMeter comes with an out-of-the-box monitoring controller. This allows you to monitor the general health of the application or web server. These include lightweight web containers such as Jetty, Apache Tomcat, Resin, or fully stacked heavy weight ones such as WebSphere, Weblogic, JBoss, Geronimo, Oracle OCJ4, and so on. Metrics such as active threads, memory, health, and load are gathered and reported in a graphical form. Having such metrics makes it easier to see the relationship between server performance and response time on the clients. Multiple servers can be monitored using a single monitor controller. Although originally designed to work with Apache Tomcat server (`http://tomcat.apache.org/`), any servlet (`http://en.wikipedia.org/wiki/Servlet_container`) container supporting **Java Management Extension (JMX)** can port the Tomcat status servlet to provide the same information. Providing such a port for other servers goes beyond the scope of this book, we will stick to using Apache Tomcat for our use case.

Monitoring servers during test executions helps identify potential bottlenecks in the application or system resource. It can draw focus to long-running queries, insufficient thread and data source pools, insufficient heap size, high I/O activity, server capacity inadequacies, slow performing application components, tracking CPU usage, and so on. All these are important in troubleshooting performance issues and attaining the targeted goals.

To get started, we first need a server to monitor. Let's download Apache Tomcat and get it up and running.

# Setting up Apache Tomcat Server

To set up Apache Tomcat Server, perform the following steps:

1. Download Apache Tomcat from `http://tomcat.apache.org/download-80.cgi`. At the time of writing this, version 8.0.15 is the latest. This is what we will use for our purposes though an older version will work just as well.

2. Get the `.zip` file or the compressed `.tar` file.

3. Extract the contents of the archive to a location of your choice. We will refer to this as `TOMCAT_HOME` for the remainder of this chapter.

4. From the command line, change to the TOMCAT_HOME/bin directory.

5. Start the server to verify that the installation is OK:

   ○ On windows, run:

   **catalina.bat run**

   ○ On unix, run:

   **./catalina.sh run**

If all goes well, the server will start up and you will see something similar to this on the console:

```
Using CATALINA_BASE:   /Users/berinle/devtools/server/apache-
tomcat-8.0.15
Using CATALINA_HOME:   /Users/berinle/devtools/server/apache-
tomcat-8.0.15
Using CATALINA_TMPDIR: /Users/berinle/devtools/server/apache-
tomcat-8.0.15/temp
Using JRE_HOME:        /Users/berinle/.jenv/versions/oracle64-1.8.0.20
Using CLASSPATH:       /Users/berinle/devtools/server/apache-
tomcat-8.0.15/bin/bootstrap.jar:/Users/berinle/devtools/server/apache-
tomcat-8.0.15/bin/tomcat-juli.jar
15-Dec-2014 14:33:32.711 INFO [main] org.apache.catalina.startup.
VersionLoggerListener.log Server version:        Apache Tomcat/8.0.15
...
15-Dec-2014 14:33:34.139 INFO [localhost-startStop-1] org.apache.
catalina.startup.HostConfig.deployDirectory Deployment of web
application directory /Users/berinle/devtools/server/apache-
tomcat-8.0.15/webapps/ROOT has finished in 31 ms
15-Dec-2014 14:33:34.143 INFO [main] org.apache.coyote.
AbstractProtocol.start Starting ProtocolHandler ["http-nio-8080"]
15-Dec-2014 14:33:34.150 INFO [main] org.apache.coyote.
AbstractProtocol.start Starting ProtocolHandler ["ajp-nio-8009"]
15-Dec-2014 14:33:34.151 INFO [main] org.apache.catalina.startup.
Catalina.start Server startup in 1119 ms
```

If the server doesn't start up, then it could be that the JAVA_HOME home is not properly set up (refer to *Chapter 1*, *Performance Testing Fundamentals* for details), or the executable files in the bin directory don't have the right permissions. Please refer to the Apache Tomcat documentation at http://tomcat.apache.org/tomcat-8.0-doc/setup.html for more details.

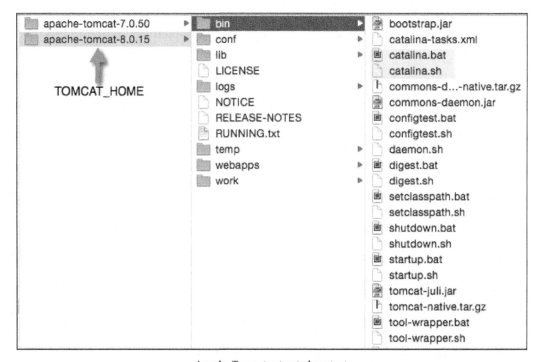

Apache Tomcat extracted content

Point your browser to `http://localhost:8080` and verify that you are greeted with the Apache Tomcat home screen.

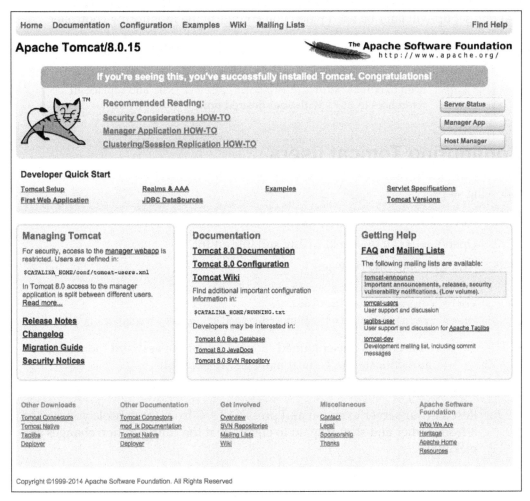

Apache Tomcat Home Screen

Congratulations, your server is now up and running! To monitor it, you need to perform one more step on the server. You need to set up at least one user account with the proper role on the server to get the information you need. The account that you set up will later be used when you configure the monitoring controller in JMeter shortly.

 To use a port other than the default 8080 Tomcat users, you will need to edit $TOMCAT_HOME/conf/server.xml and replace all references to 8080 with your desired port.

## Configuring Tomcat users

To configure the Tomcat role and the user needed for this section, perform the following steps:

1. Navigate to TOMCAT_HOME/conf.

2. Open tomcat-users.xml in any suitable editor.

3. Add the following between:
   ```
   <tomcat-users></tomcat-users>
   <role rolename="manager-gui"/>
   <user username="admin" password="admin" roles="manager-gui"/>
   ```
   ○ This creates a user named "admin" with the password "admin" to authenticate the Tomcat manager application

4. Save the file.

5. Restart your server to stop it and press *Ctrl* + *C* from the console you started it from earlier and start it again to ensure that the configuration changes are picked up.

6. Visit http://localhost:8080/manager/html.

7. Enter the login credentials (admin for both username and password) when prompted.

8. You should now be able to see the manager page.

Finally, with the server configurations behind us, we can now proceed with setting up JMeter to monitor the server.

Contents of tomcat-users.xml:

```
<?xml version='1.0' encoding='utf-8'?>
<tomcat-users>
```

```
<role rolename="manager-gui"/>
<user username="admin" password="admin" roles="manager-gui"/>
</tomcat-users>
```

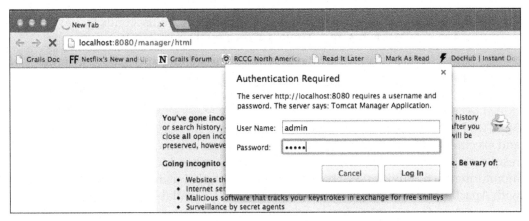

Authenticating with Tomcat Application Manager

# Setting up a monitor controller in JMeter

To set up a monitor controller in JMeter, perform the following steps:

1. Launch JMeter.

2. Add a new Thread group by navigating to **Test Plan | Add | Threads (Users) | Thread Group**.

3. Add an HTTP authorization Manager by navigating to **Thread Group | Add |Config Element | HTTP Authorization Manager**:
    ◦ Base URL: (leave blank)
    ◦ Username: admin
    ◦ Password: admin
    ◦ Domain: (leave blank)
    ◦ Realm: (leave blank)

4. Add an HTTP request by navigating to **Thread Group | Add | Sampler | HTTP Request**:
    ◦ Name: Server Status (optional)
    ◦ Server Name: localhost
    ◦ Port Number: 8080
    ◦ Path: /manager/status

5. Add a request parameter named "XML" in uppercase. Give it a value "true" in lowercase.

6. Check **Use as Monitor** at the bottom of the sampler.

7. Add a constant timer with a thread delay of 5000 milliseconds by navigating to **Thread Group | Add | Timer | Constant Timer**.

8. Add a Monitor listener by navigating to **Thread Group | Add | Listener | Monitor Results**.

9. Save the test plan.

Now we have JMeter all set up and ready to monitor the server. We can go ahead and execute the test plan now; however, we won't see too much in terms of results, since there is no activity on the server and we need to have JMeter actively monitoring such activities. We have prepared a test plan using examples that came with Apache Tomcat (basic-monitor-sampler.jmx available at https://github.com/ptwj/ptwj-code/blob/master/chap5/basic-monitor-sampler.jmx), so grab it and let's use that to put some load on the server. Assuming that you haven't changed the default server ports of Tomcat, the provided test plan will work right out the .bat file:

- Before kicking off the provided test plan, let's change the monitor test plan to loop forever, so that we can watch the server metrics as the activity continues on the server.

- For the monitor test plan, click on **Thread Group** and check the "**forever**" box for the loop count. Save the test plan.

For the constant timer in the monitor test plan, intervals shorter than 5 seconds add stress on the server. You should consult with infrastructure engineers in your company (if any) to see what an acceptable interval may be, before you configure monitoring for a production environment. As a rule of thumb, 5 seconds is a decent number.

To run the provided test plan alongside the monitoring test plan, you need to launch another instance of JMeter and open the provided test plan in it.

So without further ado, let's kick off the monitor test plan and then execute the provided test plan to put stress on the server and see the monitoring results. If it has all been set up properly, you will see that some results start to show up under the Monitor Results Listener. The Health tab might look similar to the succeeding figure Monitor Results Listener (Health Tab), and the Performance tab-like figure Monitor Results Listener (Performance Tab). As you can see, from the Monitor Results Listener (Health Tab) figure, our run gradually progressed from healthy and stopped at active at the end of the simulation run. We didn't reach the warning or dead levels, which is a good sign as our server stayed healthy overall.

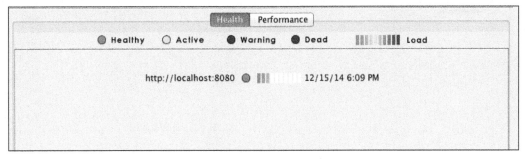

Monitor Results Listener (Health tab)

In the Monitor Results Listener (Performance Tab) figure, you can see **Memory** (represented by the yellow line), and **Load** (represented by the blue line) gradually spike up during our simulation. The **Thread** percentage (represented by the red line) and **Health** (represented by the green line) also stayed on healthy levels consistent with what we observed.

That wraps up our look into basic monitoring with JMeter. In the next section, we will see how we can leverage JMeter's plugin architecture and use a plugin to provide even granular monitoring metrics for our needs.

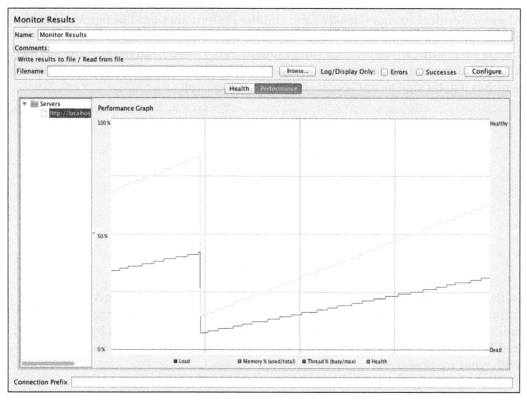

Monitor Results Listener (Performance tab)

# Monitoring the server with a JMeter plugin

So far, we have examined how we can use the built-in server monitoring capabilities of JMeter to monitor server health. While this might be OK for basic needs, it falls short for advanced needs. For instance, the graphs generated don't provide CPU and disk I/O metrics that can be deemed critical for your analysis. To get such metrics, you can extend JMeter with a suite of plugins that give better results. JMeter plugins hosted at `http://jmeter-plugins.org` is a neat project that aims to extend JMeter with some much needed features that are lacking out of the box. The project provides additional samplers, graphs, listeners, and so on, all of which make it more fun to work with JMeter. In this section, we will install this suite of plugins and use the monitoring capability it provides to get better metrics.

The only prerequisite for installing it is that you are running JMeter 2.8 or later with JRE 1.6 (Java Runtime Environment) or above.

## Installing the plugins

The plugin comes with three archives all of which must be extracted to different destinations. At the time of writing this, the project was at version 1.2.0, which is what we will be working with.

Let's try the following steps to install the plugins:

1. Navigate to the download section of `http://jmeter-plugins.org/`.

2. Download the `JMeterPlugins-Standard-1.2.0.zip` file:
   - This archive contains JMeter custom plugins

3. Download the `ServerAgent-2.2.1.zip` file:
   - This archive contains server resource monitoring agents to use with the `PerfMon Metrics Collector` plugin standalone utility

4. Extract the contents of the `JMeterPlugins-Standard-1.2.0.zip` file into `JMETER_HOME`:
   - Specifically, copy the contents of `lib/ext` from the archive into `JMETER_HOME/lib/ext`

5. Extract the contents of the `ServerAgent-2.2.1.zip` file into the `TOMCAT_HOME/serveragent` directory:
   - Be aware that you'll need to create the `serveragent` directory

6. Download the `JMeterPlugins-1.1.0.zip` file.

7. This archive contains JMeter custom plugins.

8. Download the `JMeterPlugins-libs-1.1.0.zip` file:

   ○ This archive contains additional third-party JAR's used by some of the custom plugins provided

9. Download the `ServerAgent-2.2.1.zip`.file:

   ○ This archive contains server resource monitoring agents to use with the PerfMon Metrics Collector plugin standalone utility

10. Extract the contents of the `JMeterPlugins-1.1.0.zip` file into `JMETER_HOME/lib/ext`.

11. Extract the contents of the `JMeterPlugins-libs-1.1.0.zip` file into `JMETER_HOME/lib`.

12. Extract the contents of the `ServerAgent-2.2.1.zip` file into `TOMCAT_HOME`.

With these steps, we have installed a whole suite of plugins, adding new features to JMeter. If you were to relaunch JMeter now, you will notice additional samplers, listeners, timers, and so on, all beginning with jp@gc to distinguish them from the bundled ones.

Let's start the server agent, which will feed the JMeter listener probe that we will add to our test plan later.

We will begin with the following steps:

1. Start shell or DOS prompt.

2. Navigate to the `TOMCAT_HOME/serveragent` directory.

3. Start the agent:

   ○ On Windows, run:

   **startAgent.bat**

   ○ On Unix, run:

   **./startAgent.sh**

You should see logs similar to the following ones if the agent has started successfully:

```
INFO      2015-01-05 19:13:33.328 [kg.apc.p] (): Binding UDP to 4444
INFO      2015-01-05 19:13:34.329 [kg.apc.p] (): Binding TCP to 4444
INFO      2015-01-05 19:13:34.334 [kg.apc.p] (): JP@GC Agent v2.2.0
started
```

As you can see, the agent has started on port 4444, the default. We will use this port later when configuring the monitor listener for JMeter. If this port is not satisfactory for you, the plugin provides configuration files that can be edited to choose a desired port. Please refer to the documentation at http://jmeter-plugins.org/.

With the server agent running, let's add a few monitor listeners to our test plan. For our purposes, we have chosen the sample test plan we recorded using the samples provided by Apache Tomcat.

 Please note that these same concepts can be applied to other applications deployed on the same server where the monitor agent has been installed.

# Adding monitor listeners to the test plan

To add a monitor listener to the test plan, perform the following steps:

1. Launch JMeter.
2. Open the test plan provided (advanced-monitoring-sampler-1.jmx, https://github.com/ptwj/ptwj-code/blob/master/chap5/advanced-monitoring-sampler-1.jmx).
3. Add a PerfMon Metrics Collector listener by navigating to **Test Plan | Add | Listener | jp@gc – PerfMon Metrics Collector**:
    ◦ Add one row each to gather these metrics (**CPU**, **Memory**, **Network I/O, Disks I/O**)
    ◦ **Host/IP: localhost**
    ◦ **Port: 4444**
    ◦ Metrics to collect (dropdown): **CPU/Memory/Network I/O, Disks I/O**
4. Add a response time vs threads listener by navigating to **Test Plan | Add | Listener | jp@gc – Response Times over Time**.
5. Add a Transactions per second listener by navigating to **Test Plan | Add | Listener | jp@gc – Transactions per Second**.
6. Save the test plan.

With the server agent running, and our additional monitor listeners set up, we are ready to kick off the simulation execution. Let's go right on and execute it. While it's executing, we can see the graphical representation of the metrics we have chosen to analyze if you click on the **jp@gc - PerfMon Metrics Collector**. As you can see from the PerfMon Metrics Collector figure, the CPU is spiking up and down, showing quite a descent load on the server. The memory stays almost constant while the network, relatively stable, spiked quite high two minutes into our simulation run. It immediately dropped down back to the low ranges after the spike, so something might have transpired on the network at the time of the execution run, causing such a spike. Since this test plan doesn't involve any disk I/O, it stays on 0 for the duration of our simulation.

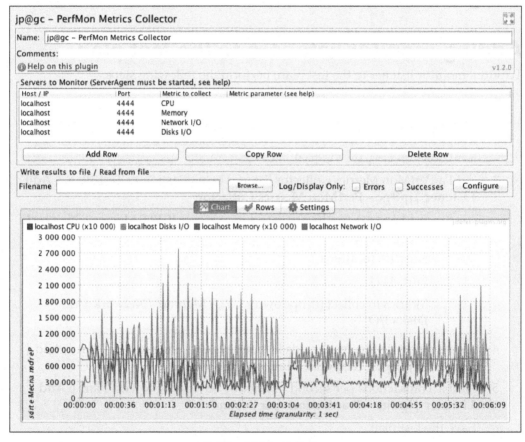

PerfMon Metrics Collector

The response time over time listener shows a true picture of how much time the server takes to service each request over the elapsed time of the simulation run. The graph can be a bit clobbered to read, so in the "Rows" tab, you can check only the requests you are interested in analyzing. We have done just this in the response times vs threads figure, and chosen only a handful of requests. As you can see, we have an elapsed time of a little over three minutes and the highest response time from this graph was for request /examples at about the 1:32 and 1:50 mark.

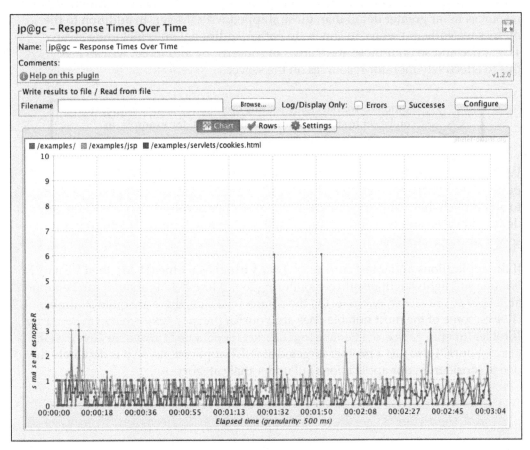

Response Times vs. Threads

Though the graph isn't shown here, the last listener we added was the Transactions per Second Listener. It shows just how many requests (transactions) the server was able to handle during the course of our simulation run on a second-by-second basis. Like the Response times over time listener, the chart can be clobbered and you will need to selectively choose which requests you were interested in to make some sense of the graph.

As you can see, these new listeners along with the server agent allow you to monitor resources in far greater detail than those shipped with JMeter. In addition to the metrics we gathered, you can choose to gather additional ones including swap, TCP, JMX, and so on if those were areas of concern. By and large, we can use this to effectively monitor resources on the server.

 Although we have only set this up for one server, the monitor can be set up to monitor multiple servers, for example, in cases where we have a cluster of servers.

We have just scratched the surface of how servers can be monitored during performance testing and since this is a book about JMeter, we are sticking to how to accomplish the task using it. However, for deeper monitoring needs, there are dedicated tools both free and commercial that do a much more thorough job at server resource analysis.

If the applications under test run on the **Java Virtual Machine (JVM)**, then VisualVM is a free and lightweight resource-monitoring tool. More details about it can be found at http://visualvm.java.net. On the commercial side, there are quite a number of choices; some of the most notable ones are YourKit (http://www.yourkit.com/) and JProfiler (https://www.ej-technologies.com/products/jprofiler/overview. html). YourKit also has a profiler targeted at .NET applications, so it is definitely the one to consider if your applications fall under that category.

# Summary

In this chapter, we walked through how JMeter can help with monitoring server resources. To do this, we set up an Apache Tomcat server to monitor. Once done, we examined the built-in capabilities of JMeter with regards to monitoring. We further examined how we can get more granular monitoring metrics by extending JMeter with custom-developed plugins. This allowed us to monitor server resources such as CPU, disk I/O, memory, and network I/O among other things. Through the plugin, we also got additional samplers, timers, processors, and listeners that allowed us to monitor transactions per second and response over time metrics. Though not an extensive monitoring tool, JMeter proved itself as a capable tool to do basic monitoring of server resources.

In the next chapter, we will go in depth on distributed testing and see how to leverage the capabilities of JMeter to accomplish this.

# 6

# Distributed Testing

There will come a time when running your test plans on a single machine won't cut it any longer performance-wise, since resources on the single box are limited. For example, this can be the case when you want to spin-off a thousand users for a test plan. Depending on the power and resources of the machine you are testing on and the nature of your test plans, a single machine can probably spin-off with 300–600 threads before starting to error out or causing inaccurate test results. There are several reasons why this may happen. One is because there is a limit to the amount of threads you can spin-off on a single machine. Most operating systems guard against complete system failure by placing such limits on hosted applications. Also, your use case may require you to simulate requests from various IP addresses. Distributed testing allows you to replicate tests across many low-end machines, enabling you to start more threads and thereby simulating more load on the server. In this chapter, we will learn how to leverage JMeter for distributed testing and put more load on the server under test in the process.

## Remote testing with JMeter

JMeter has inbuilt support for distributed testing. This enables a single JMeter GUI instance known as the *master*, to control a number of remote JMeter instances, known as *slaves* and collect all the test results from them. The features offered by this approach are as follows:

- Saving of test samples to the local machine
- Managing multiple instances of **JMeterEngine** (slave nodes) from a single machine
- Replicating the test plan from the master node to each controlled server without the need to copy them to each server

Distributed Testing

[  JMeter does not distribute the load between servers. Each server
will execute the same test plan in its entirety. ]

Though the test plan is replicated across to each server, the data needed by the test
plan, if any, is not. In cases where input data such as CSV data is needed to run the
tests, such data needs to be made available on each server where the test plan will
be executed. This can be a shared network mount that all the servers can get to.

[  The remote mode is more resource intensive than running the same
number of non-GUI tests independently. If many server instances are
used, the client's JMeter can become overloaded, as can the client's
network connection, since results need to be communicated in real
time from the slave to the master. ]

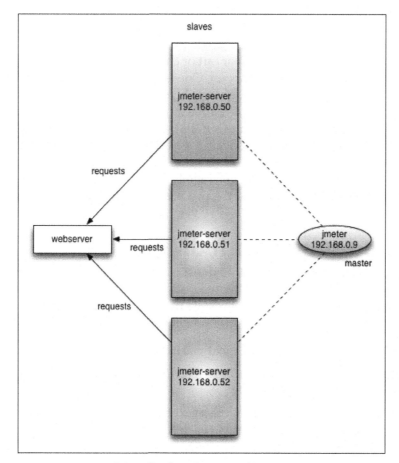

JMeter distributed testing architecture

[ 90 ]

It is important that all the slave nodes and the master node are running the same version of JMeter and if possible, the same version of Java Runtime Environment. Mostly, minor JRE variations are fine but not major ones. For example, master could be running on JRE 1.6.12 and slaves on 1.6.17, but not 1.6.xx versus 1.5.xx.

# Configuring JMeter slave nodes

There are a number of ways to get the slave nodes going. In this section, we will go over two options that will often fit the bill for accomplishing your goals.

The most obvious is to go out and buy new machines just for this purpose. For most of us, that is not feasible. Another option is to get hold of extra computers lying around in the office, configure them appropriately, and use them for this purpose. While that will work perfectly, it may be time consuming to get all the boxes set up without the appropriate tools, knowledge, and expertise. Another option is to use virtual machines to accomplish the same. This is the option we will be focusing on in this section. We favor this approach for the following reasons:

- We don't necessarily need another physical machine to try out distributed testing
- We can leverage **Vagrant** an excellent infrastructure automation tool (https://www.vagrantup.com) to set up virtual boxes with needed software with little interaction from us
- We can be up and running with a few virtual machines in less time than it takes to run to your local coffee shop and grab a cup of coffee
- It is free
- It can be used with configuration management tools such as Puppet, Chef, Ansible, and Salt
- The same concepts can be applied to leverage machines in the cloud (AWS, Rackspace, Digital Ocean, and so on) to test

In case you haven't heard of Vagrant before, don't be alarmed. It's an excellent tool that makes building development environments easy. It allows you to create and configure lightweight, reproducible, and portable development environments. Elaborating on the uses of Vagrant go beyond the scope of this book, but I'll encourage you to read more about them at http://www.vagrantup.com. Grab a copy of Vagrant at https://www.vagrantup.com/downloads.html. At the time of writing, version 1.7.2 is the latest, and that is what we will be using in this chapter.

For this book, we prepared the necessary scripts you can use to provision boxes. The only requirement to use the script is to have Oracle's **VirtualBox** installed on your machine. VirtualBox comes with installers for Windows, Mac OS, Solaris, and Linux. You can grab a copy of the operating system of your choice at `https://www.virtualbox.org/wiki/Downloads`. At the time of writing, VirtualBox is at Version 4.3.20, and that is what we installed.

With both Vagrant and VirtualBox installed, we are ready to configure our distributed testing environment. Let's go right ahead and do that.

# Configuring one slave per machine

In this configuration, we are going to set up three slave machines and control them with one master client. This will mimic having four separate physical machines with one of them acting as master (where the JMeter GUI client runs) and the other three machines acting as slave nodes (where the JMeter server scripts are kicked-off). Perform the following steps:

1. Download the Vagrant project provided for this section from `https://github.com/ptwj/slave_master/archive/master.zip`.
2. Extract the contents to a folder of your choice, for example, `ch6_01`.
3. On the command line, go to the extracted folder.
4. Run `vagrant up n1`.
5. If prompted, choose the appropriate connection to bridge. If you are on a wireless connection, for example, choose **en1: Wi-Fi**. If you are on Ethernet, choose **en0: Ethernet**, and so on.

In a few moments, a fully functional VirtualBox will be created with JMeter installed and ready to run! You should see logs similar to the following:

```
Bringing machine 'n1' up with 'virtualbox' provider...
==> n1: Importing base box 'ubuntu/trusty64'...
==> n1: Matching MAC address for NAT networking...
==> n1: Checking if box 'ubuntu/trusty64' is up to date...
==> n1: Setting the name of the VM: vagrant_slave_master_
n1_1422016178879_40938
==> n1: Clearing any previously set forwarded ports...
==> n1: Clearing any previously set network interfaces...
==> n1: Preparing network interfaces based on configuration...
    n1: Adapter 1: nat
    n1: Adapter 2: hostonly
```

```
==> n1: Forwarding ports...
    n1: 22 => 2222 (adapter 1)
==> n1: Booting VM...
==> n1: Waiting for machine to boot. This may take a few minutes...
...
```

Don't take our word for it though. Verify that the box is properly configured by performing the following on the command line (from the same folder you ran `vagrant up n1` from):

```
vagrant ssh n1
```

```
cd /opt/apache-jmeter-2.12/bin
```

```
./jmeter --version
```

This should show you the version of JMeter that you are running on the guest machine. In my case, as you can see in the following log, it reports `Version 2.12 r1636949`:

```
vagrant@trusty64:~$ cd /opt/apache-jmeter-2.12/bin

vagrant@trusty64:/opt/apache-jmeter-2.12/bin$ ./jmeter --version

log_file=jmeter.log java.io.FileNotFoundException: jmeter.log (Permission
denied)

[log_file-> System.out]

2015/01/23 12:36:31 INFO  - jmeter.util.JMeterUtils: Setting Locale to
en_US

2015/01/23 12:36:31 INFO  - jmeter.JMeter: Loading user properties from:
/opt/apache-jmeter-2.12/bin/user.properties

2015/01/23 12:36:31 INFO  - jmeter.JMeter: Loading system properties
from: /opt/apache-jmeter-2.12/bin/system.properties

2015/01/23 12:36:31 INFO  - jmeter.JMeter: Copyright (c) 1998-2014 The
Apache Software Foundation

2015/01/23 12:36:31 INFO  - jmeter.JMeter: Version 2.12 r1636949

2015/01/23 12:36:31 INFO  - jmeter.JMeter: java.version=1.7.0_65

2015/01/23 12:36:31 INFO  - jmeter.JMeter: java.vm.name=OpenJDK 64-Bit
Server VM

2015/01/23 12:36:31 INFO  - jmeter.JMeter: os.name=Linux

2015/01/23 12:36:31 INFO  - jmeter.JMeter: os.arch=amd64

2015/01/23 12:36:31 INFO  - jmeter.JMeter: os.version=3.13.0-44-generic

2015/01/23 12:36:31 INFO  - jmeter.JMeter: file.encoding=UTF-8

2015/01/23 12:36:31 INFO  - jmeter.JMeter: Default Locale=English (United
States)
```

```
2015/01/23 12:36:31 INFO  - jmeter.JMeter: JMeter  Locale=English (United
States)

2015/01/23 12:36:31 INFO  - jmeter.JMeter: JMeterHome=/opt/apache-
jmeter-2.12

2015/01/23 12:36:31 INFO  - jmeter.JMeter: user.dir  =/opt/apache-
jmeter-2.12/bin

2015/01/23 12:36:31 INFO  - jmeter.JMeter: PWD        =/opt/apache-
jmeter-2.12/bin

2015/01/23 12:36:31 INFO  - jmeter.JMeter: IP: 127.0.1.1 Name: trusty64
FullName: trusty64

Copyright (c) 1998-2014 The Apache Software Foundation

Version 2.12 r1636949
```

We provisioned our JMeter installation to reside at `/opt/apache-jmeter-2.12`. For the rest of this section, we'll refer to this location (`/opt/apache-jmeter-2.12`) as `JMETER_HOME`.

If we attempt to kick-off JMeter server on this node now (from `apache-jmeter-2.12/bin` directory, run `./jmeter-server`), we will encounter an error like the following:

```
vagrant@trusty64:/opt/apache-jmeter-2.12/bin$ ./jmeter-server

2015/01/23 12:40:50 INFO  - jmeter.engine.RemoteJMeterEngineImpl:
Starting backing engine on 1099

2015/01/23 12:40:50 INFO  - jmeter.engine.RemoteJMeterEngineImpl: Local
IP address=127.0.1.1

Server failed to start: java.rmi.RemoteException: Cannot start. trusty64
is a loopback address.

2015/01/23 12:40:50 ERROR - jmeter.JMeter: Giving up, as server failed
with: java.rmi.RemoteException: Cannot start. trusty64 is a loopback
address.
```

This is because the server is returning an IP address of `127.0.1.1` that is considered a loop back address. To fix this, we need to find out the assigned IP address of the virtual machine and edit `$JMETER_HOME/bin/jmeter-server` to add that IP address. To get the assigned IP address from the newly created virtual machine, run this on the command line:

```
ifconfig | grep inet
```

The line of interest here is the line containing 192.168.x.x or 172.x.x.x depending on your network. For our node, the assigned IP address is 172.28.128.3:

```
inet addr:10.0.2.15  Bcast:10.0.2.255  Mask:255.255.255.0
          inet6 addr: fe80::a00:27ff:fe26:6cc6/64 Scope:Link
          inet addr:172.28.128.3  Bcast:172.28.128.255
Mask:255.255.255.0
          inet6 addr: fe80::a00:27ff:feda:ecbc/64 Scope:Link
          inet addr:127.0.0.1  Mask:255.0.0.0
          inet6 addr: ::1/128 Scope:Host
```

Now edit $JMETER_HOME/bin/jmeter-server using an editor of choice. Vim comes with the virtual machine we just created, so edit the file using the command vi $JMETER_HOME/bin/jmeter-server. Look for the line beginning with RMI_HOST_DEF and add the following just below it:

```
    RMI_HOST_DEF=-Djava.rmi.server.hostname=172.28.128.3
```

 Be sure to replace the 172.28.128.3 here with the assigned IP address of your own virtual box.

Save the file (by pressing *Esc*, then typing :wq) and this machine is ready to act as a server. Before we configure a second node, it would be wise to take it for a spin. Let's run JMETER_HOME/bin/jmeter-server again on the machine. This time, it should succeed and you should see something similar to the following on the console:

```
Created remote object: UnicastServerRef [liveRef:
[endpoint:[192.168.1.27:46313](local),objID:[62a8e304:13da47c073a:-7fff,
-369620866826328728]]]
```

Now, it is waiting for instructions from the master. Let's go right ahead and configure the master to control it.

## Configuring the master node

Now that we have one slave node configured, we can test it out by configuring the master node to connect to it and control it. To do that, we will have to add the slave node's IP address to the master's node configuration file.

On the host machine (where JMeter GUI client is running), perform the following steps:

1.  Open JMETER_HOME/bin/jmeter.properties.
2.  Look for the line beginning with remote_hosts=127.0.0.1.

3. Change it to `remote_hosts=172.28.128.3`.

4. `172.28.128.3` should be changed to match the assigned IP address of your virtual box.

5. Save the file.

6. Launch **JMeter**.

7. Navigate to **Run | Remote Start | Slave IP address** (where **Slave IP address** is the assigned IP address of your virtual machine).

By clicking on the **Slave IP address**, the master node will make a connection with the remote server running on the VirtualBox. You will see a similar log on the client and the server, respectively:

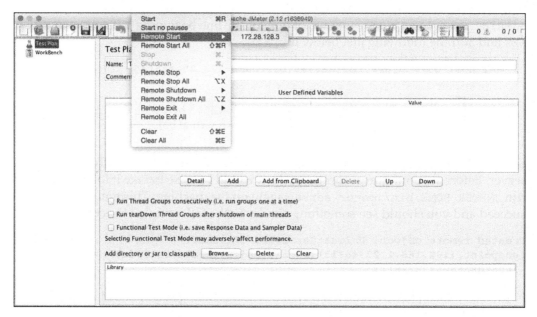

Remote Start menu

On JMeter GUI client console:

```
Using remote object: UnicastRef [liveRef: [endpoint:[172.28.128.3:60883]
(remote),objID:[-7854a167:14b16e354ea:-7fff, 2799922095106363247]]]
```

On JMeter server console:

```
Starting the test on host 172.28.128.3 @ Fri Jan 23 13:16:57 UTC 2015
(1422019017345)
```

```
Finished the test on host 172.28.128.3 @ Fri Jan 23 13:16:57 UTC 2015
(1422019017642)
```

Congratulations! We are now able to control this slave node from the master. We can proceed with testing at this point, but since we are focusing on distributed testing in this chapter, it will help to have two or more nodes to control.

Repeat the same steps we used to configure node_one, to spin-off two more nodes node_two and node_three. To spin-off the second and third slave machines, run vagrant up n2 and vagrant up n3, respectively. Once the machines are up, add their assigned IP addresses to jmeter.properties of the master node like we did for node_one. In the end, we should have three slave nodes, which we can now control from the master node.

Now your JMeter GUI client should have three server IP addresses under **Run | Remote Start**, and you can either kick-off an individual server node by targeting the server IP address of choice, or start all configured slave nodes at once by navigating to **Run | Remote Start All** (*Command + Shift + R* on Mac or *Ctrl + Shift + R* on Windows). When starting all the configured node servers, if everything has been properly configured, you should see logs similar to the following on the master console with each server node responding and acknowledging, kicking-off the intended test plan:

```
Using remote object: UnicastRef [liveRef: [endpoint:[ 172.28.128.3:60883]
(remote),objID:[49a18727:13da4a8a955:-7fff, -4630561463080329291]]]
```

```
Using remote object: UnicastRef [liveRef: [endpoint:[ 172.28.128.5:51200]
(remote),objID:[46a1e04c:13da4a79d3d:-7fff, -5213066472819797239]]]
```

```
Using remote object: UnicastRef [liveRef: [endpoint:[ 172.28.128.6:51791]
(remote),objID:[-1434b37d:13da4a85f8a:-7fff, -2658534524006849789]]]
```

As you can see from the preceding logs, the master node makes connection with all the three configured slave nodes 172.28.128.3, 172.28.128.5, and 172.28.128.6. With the connections verified, we can now pick a test plan to run and gather the results on the master node.

For our first test, we are going to execute a test that doesn't require input data. The provided test plan (https://raw.githubusercontent.com/ptwj/ptwj-code/master/chap6/browse-apple-itunes.jmx) navigates to Apple's iTunes website and browses around a bit for music, movies, apps, and so on. It does no data entry and therefore doesn't need any input data. Load that into the master node's JMeter GUI and kick-it-off on all slave nodes. The script launches 150 users over 30 seconds and runs for two iterations. Since we are distributing this over three slave nodes, we will have a total of 450 users launched (150 users per node) and 15 users started per second, that is, 450/30. The following are the results our machine produced. It's a quad-core MacBook Pro with a 2.2GHz processor and 8GB of RAM. Your mileage may vary depending on the computing power of your machine:

| Label | # Samples | Average | Median | 90% Line | Min | Max | Error % | Throughput | KB/sec |
|---|---|---|---|---|---|---|---|---|---|
| Apple Home | 900 | 1321 | 857 | 2554 | 518 | 7695 | 0.00% | 8.6/sec | 630.4 |
| iTunes | 900 | 1104 | 772 | 2083 | 542 | 5524 | 0.11% | 8.6/sec | 204.2 |
| Featured | 900 | 637 | 450 | 1321 | 336 | 5086 | 0.00% | 8.9/sec | 116.0 |
| Songs | 900 | 715 | 470 | 1676 | 329 | 12980 | 0.00% | 8.0/sec | 132.8 |
| Albums | 900 | 200 | 63 | 327 | 18 | 4607 | 0.00% | 8.1/sec | 108.5 |
| TV Shows | 900 | 672 | 436 | 1766 | 308 | 4895 | 0.00% | 8.0/sec | 132.1 |
| Movies | 900 | 214 | 56 | 317 | 18 | 12474 | 0.00% | 8.1/sec | 95.8 |
| Movie Rentals | 900 | 217 | 57 | 317 | 19 | 12429 | 0.00% | 8.1/sec | 102.0 |
| Free Apps | 900 | 267 | 61 | 428 | 16 | 12574 | 0.00% | 8.1/sec | 99.1 |
| Paid Apps | 900 | 322 | 62 | 832 | 17 | 4700 | 0.00% | 8.1/sec | 99.9 |
| Music Videos | 900 | 371 | 72 | 1014 | 17 | 12668 | 0.00% | 8.2/sec | 108.5 |
| TOTAL | 9900 | 549 | 341 | 1502 | 16 | 12980 | 0.01% | 76.6/sec | 1524.9 |

Aggregate report for Browse Apple iTunes distributed test

 It should be noted that in our case, we are still running all these virtual slave nodes on a single box, so the resources are still limited. That is, all the slaves are still sharing the resource of the host machine. Therefore, attempting to distribute more load than that can be originally handled by the host machine can lead to degraded performance with high response times. However, nothing prevents you from running the provided Vagrant scripts on additional physical machines to simulate more load without worrying about constrained resources.

The second test is one we have seen before in *Chapter 2, Recording Your First Test*. It's the Excilys' banking application that requires an input data file. As JMeter only sends the test plans to slave nodes, we need to get the input files across to all slave nodes in other to successfully execute the test. To do that, perform the following steps:

1. On the command line, go to the directory of the slave node.

2. Run the following commands in sequence:

3. SSH into the machine

   ```
   vagrant ssh
   ```

4.  Go to the JMeter bin directory

    ```
    cd apache-jmeter-2.12/bin
    ```

5.  Get the `users2.txt` file from a remote location:

    ```
    wget https://raw.github.com/berinle/vagrant-data/master/users2.txt
    ```

Repeat the steps for all three nodes. This puts the `users2.txt` file, that is needed by the test plan, in a location that can be seen by the JMeter server on the slave nodes. Now open the test plan (`exilys-bank-scenario-2.jmx`) on the master JMeter GUI client. As before, select **Run | Remote Start All**. Feel free to increase the number of threads, ramp-up, and iterations, but please be careful not to crash the server.

# Configuring multiple slave nodes on a single box

JMeter allows you to configure multiple slave nodes on a single box as long as they are configured to broadcast on different RMI ports. This can come in handy in cases where the machine you are using is powerful enough to handle it or you don't have access to additional physical machines. Just like in the previous section, we will be using Vagrant to configure a single virtual machine and spin-off multiple JMeter slave nodes on it. For this illustration, we prepared a Vagrant script with shell provisioning, similar to what we had in the last section. This brings up a VirtualBox, exposes port 1099 (standard JMeter RMI port), 1664, and 1665, and installs three JMeter slave nodes named `jmeter-1`, `jmeter-2`, and `jmeter-3`, respectively. These are the different ports that will be used by the different slave nodes when starting the server. To get started, proceed with the following steps:

1.  Download the bundle from this section from `https://github.com/ptwj/adhoc_distributed/archive/master.zip` and into a directory of your choice. We will call it VAGRANT_EXTRACT.

2.  From the command line, go to the VAGRANT_EXTRACT directory.

3.  Run `vagrant up`.

4.  If prompted, choose the appropriate connection to bridge. If you are on a wireless connection, for example, choose `en1: Wi-Fi`. If you are on Ethernet, choose `en0: Ethernet`, and so on.

5.  Wait for the VirtualBox to be fully built.

6.  Run `vagrant ssh`.

7.  Run `cd /opt`

8.  Run `ls -1`.

At this point, you should see the three slave nodes present on the machine as follows:

```
vagrant@trusty64:/opt$ ls -la
drwxr-xr-x  5 root     root 4096 Jan 23 14:42 .
drwxr-xr-x 23 root     root 4096 Jan 23 14:40 ..
drwxr-xr-x  8 vagrant root 4096 Jan 23 14:42 jmeter-1
drwxr-xr-x  8 vagrant root 4096 Jan 23 14:42 jmeter-2
drwxr-xr-x  8 vagrant root 4096 Jan 23 14:42 jmeter-3
```

The only thing left now is to configure `RMI_HOST_DEF` in `JMETER_HOME/bin/jmeter-server`, as we did in the previous section to avoid the loop back error that will be reported. From the VirtualBox, run the following on the command line:

```
ifconfig | grep inet
```

This will provide you the assigned IP address of the box.

Edit the `jmeter-server` script to add the box IP address using the following steps:

1. Run `vi /opt/jmeter-1/bin/jmeter-server`.
2. Look for the line beginning with `#RMI_HOST_DEF` and replace it with `RMI_HOST_DEF=-Djava.rmi.server.hostname=172.28.128.3` (replacing `172.28.128.3` with the assigned IP address of your virtual box).
3. Save and close the file (press *Esc*, type `:wq`).
4. Repeat the process for the other two slave nodes (`jmeter-2` and `jmeter-3`).

At this point, the slave nodes are ready to be kicked-off, and the only thing left to do is to start each of them up on our already configured RMI ports (1099, 1664, and 1665).

To start the `jmeter-1` slave node in a new shell/console, perform the following steps:

1. Go to the `VAGRANT_EXTRACT` directory.

   ```
   cd VAGRANT_EXTRACT.
   ```

2. SSH into the box.

   ```
   vagrant ssh
   ```

3. Start the JMeter server on the default port: 1099.

   ```
   cd /opt/jmeter-1 && ./bin/jmeter-server
   ```

To start the `jmeter-2` slave node in a new shell/console, perform the following steps:

1. Go to the `VAGRANT_EXTRACT` directory.

   **`cd VAGRANT_EXTRACT`**

2. SSH into the box.

   **`vagrant ssh`**

3. Start the JMeter server on port 1664.

   **`cd /opt/jmeter-2 && SERVER_PORT=1664 ./bin/jmeter-server`**

To start the `jmeter-3` slave node in a new shell/console, perform the following steps:

1. Go to the `VAGRANT_EXTRACT` directory.

   **`cd VAGRANT_EXTRACT`**

2. SSH into the box.

   **`vagrant ssh`**

3. Start the JMeter server on port 1665.

   **`cd /opt/jmeter-3 && SERVER_PORT=1665 ./bin/jmeter-server`**

# Configuring the master node

With the slave nodes configured, we will need to configure the master node to communicate with them before we can proceed with executing our tests remotely. To do that, we will have to add the slave nodes' IP addresses and ports to the master's node configuration file.

On the host machine (where JMeter GUI client is running), perform the following steps:

1. Open `JMETER_HOME/bin/jmeter.properties`.
2. Look for the line beginning with `remote_hosts=127.0.0.1` and then:
   - Change it to `remote_hosts=172.28.128.3:1099, 172.28.128.3:1664,172.28.128.3:1665`
   - `172.28.128.3` should be changed to match the assigned IP address of your VirtualBox
3. Save the file (press *Esc*, type `:wq`).
4. Launch **JMeter**.
5. Navigate to **Run | Remote Start | Slave IP address** (where **Slave IP address** is the assigned IP address of your virtual machine).

With that done, we are ready to kick-off our tests like we did in the previous section. The only difference now is that all our slave nodes are now configured on one virtual host. Open up the `browse-apple-itunes.jmx` test plan in the JMeter GUI client on the master. Change the number of threads from 150 to 15. Now, kick-off the test remotely on all the slave nodes. The test should complete after a while (be patient). If you compare the results of this run with the previous run that had slaves configured on separate virtual boxes, you will see quite an increase in the response times. The following are the results we got from our run:

| Label | # Samples | Average | Median | 90% Line | Min | Max | Error % | Throughput | KB/sec |
|---|---|---|---|---|---|---|---|---|---|
| Apple Home | 90 | 2519 | 1857 | 3170 | 564 | 16798 | 0.00% | 41.3/min | 50.4 |
| iTunes | 90 | 2365 | 1814 | 3899 | 611 | 9138 | 0.00% | 43.8/min | 17.5 |
| Featured | 90 | 1333 | 1083 | 2203 | 329 | 9340 | 0.00% | 45.9/min | 10.0 |
| Songs | 90 | 1948 | 1285 | 2880 | 320 | 18510 | 0.00% | 46.7/min | 13.0 |
| Albums | 90 | 570 | 473 | 1211 | 20 | 1674 | 0.00% | 47.6/min | 11.2 |
| TV Shows | 90 | 1243 | 1116 | 2120 | 322 | 3445 | 0.00% | 47.7/min | 13.5 |
| Movies | 90 | 600 | 471 | 1214 | 19 | 5291 | 0.00% | 48.5/min | 9.6 |
| Movie Rentals | 90 | 521 | 474 | 1088 | 22 | 1655 | 0.00% | 48.9/min | 9.7 |
| Free Apps | 90 | 696 | 409 | 1113 | 20 | 15982 | 0.00% | 49.2/min | 10.1 |
| Paid Apps | 90 | 604 | 315 | 1089 | 23 | 12594 | 0.00% | 49.6/min | 10.1 |
| Music Videos | 90 | 497 | 375 | 1126 | 19 | 1537 | 0.00% | 50.1/min | 11.1 |
| TOTAL | 990 | 1172 | 818 | 2268 | 19 | 18510 | 0.00% | 7.0/sec | 140.7 |

Aggregate report for Browse Apple iTunes distributed test 2

You can see that we observe a higher response times in the **90% Line** column for this run when compared with the previous run, even though this test is using far fewer users (15 compared to 150). One conclusion that can be drawn from these results is that spinning-off multiple slave nodes on a machine is not always optimal and should not be your first pick. Your mileage may vary based on the capacity of the machine you use.

# Leveraging the cloud for distributed testing

So far, we have seen how we can distribute load to various physical or virtual machines and by doing so achieve more load than can ever be possible with a single machine. Our setup so far, though, has been internal to our network using a master/slave configuration. Sometimes, it helps to isolate any artificial bottlenecks occurring on the LAN and run your tests from more realistic locations external to your network. This has the added benefit of leveraging substantially large hardware at minimal cost thanks to the various cloud offerings now at our disposal. Another area worth considering is the master/slave setup that we employed up to now.

While this will work perfectly well when few slaves are configured, as more slaves get added to the mix, the master node becomes a huge bottleneck. This shouldn't come as a surprise since I/O and network operations increase as more and more slave nodes try to feed ongoing testing results to the master. What will be most efficient and ideal is to have each slave node run its test in isolation in non-GUI mode, save the results, and have the cumulative results from all slave nodes gathered at the end of the test. The challenge here, of course, is kicking-off all test executions on all nodes in harmony and gathering the results from each. That can be a little bit daunting not to mention time consuming. Thankfully, we can use Vagrant, our Swiss-Army-knife environmental setup tool, to get part way there. We will employ it to start server instances on **Amazon Web Service (AWS)**, set up **Java Runtime Environment (JRE)**, JMeter, and upload our test scripts to the cloud virtual machines we bring up. Amazon has an excellent variety of cloud services that make it easy to run your whole company's infrastructure in the cloud, if you choose. Read more about it at http://aws.amazon.com/.

Provided that the application under test is accessible from outside your corperate network, the methods described here should suit your needs just fine.

The first step is to register for an AWS account, if you don't already have one. You can do that by going to http://aws.amazon.com/ and clicking on the **Sign up** button. Once registered, you'll need to obtain your access key, secret key, and a key pair to use for authenticating with the machines you create on AWS.

# Obtaining your access key, secret key, and key pair

To obtain AWS access keys, which are needed for sections in *Chapter 5, Resource Monitoring*, perform the following steps:

1. Create a free AWS Account if you don't already have one by going to http://aws.amazon.com/ and clicking on the **Sign up** or **Create a Free Account** button.

2. Once your account has been created, go to the IAM console at https://console.aws.amazon.com/iam/home?#home.

3. Click on the **Users** link on the side bar.

4. Select your IAM username and **User Actions | Manage Access Keys**:

   ° If your username does not yet exist, create a new one by clicking on the **Create New Users** button and follow the on-screen instructions.

   ° Note the Access Key ID and Secret Access Key of the newly created user and download them.

5. Click on the **Create Access Key** button:
   ° A new key/secret pair is generated and can be downloaded.

6. Click on the **Download Credentials** button. See the following screenshot for details.

7. Keep the downloaded file in a secure location as you will need that to access the instances you spin up.

8. With all that done, we are ready to start launching some instances in the cloud!

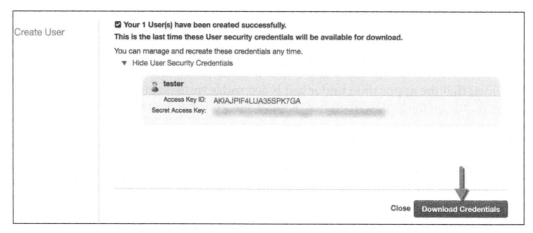

Obtaining AWS credentials

> AWS is a paid service and you are billed for every hour you have an instance up and running. At the time of writing, a small instance that we use during the course of this section, costs $0.10/hr for each instance which is not bad considering all the effort it saves; getting a box, setting it up, and doing that multiple times.

We prepared a Vagrant script with Puppet provisioning like we did in the previous sections. The only difference this time is that is it configured to work with AWS as opposed to virtual boxes in our intranet. To use it, you need to install the Vagrant AWS plugin. Do that by running the following from the command line:

```
vagrant plugin install vagrant-aws
```

This simple one liner makes Vagrant AWS aware how to interact with machines on AWS. We can now transparently spin-off virtual machines on Amazon's infrastructure like we did with VirtualBox locally.

Running the `vagrant plugin install` command, assumes that you already installed Vagrant on the machine where this operation is performed. If you haven't, please grab a copy at `https://www.vagrantup.com/downloads.html` and proceed with the installation as directed.

# Launching the AWS instance

With the Vagrant AWS plugin installed, the next step is to perform the following steps:

1. Download the prepared Vagrant bundle for this section from `https://github.com/ptwj/diy_cloud_distribution/archive/master.zip`.

2. Extract it to a location of your choice. We will refer to this as `INSTANCE_HOME`.

3. Open the `$INSTANCE_HOME/Vagrant` file in an editor of your choice and fill in the required entries:
   - `aws.secret_access_key = "YOUR AWS SECRET KEY"`
   - `aws.keypair_name= "YOUR KEYPAIR NAME"`
   - `aws.ssh_private_key_path = "PATH TO YOUR PRIVATE KEY"`
   - `aws.region = "YOUR AWS REGION"`

   (These are values as generated in the previous section *Obtain your access key, secret key, and key pair*.)

4. Save your changes.

5. From the command line, go to the directory of `INSTANCE_HOME`:
   ```
   cd $INSTANCE_HOME
   ```

6. Bring up the first virtual machine on AWS:
   ```
   vagrant up vm1 --provider=aws
   ```

7. Wait for the process to complete. You will see a bunch of entries (similar to what follows) written to the console, and the whole process could take up to a minute or two depending on network latency, internet speed, and communication with AWS among others:
   ```
   Bringing machine 'vm1' up with 'aws' provider...
   [vm1] Warning! The AWS provider doesn't support any of the Vagrant
   high-level network configurations (`config.vm.network`). They
   will be silently ignored.
   [vm1] Launching an instance with the following settings...
   ```

```
[vm1]   -- Type: m1.small
[vm1]   -- AMI: ami-7747d01e
[vm1]   -- Region: us-east-1
[vm1]   -- SSH Port: 22
[vm1]   -- Keypair: book-test
[vm1] Waiting for instance to become "ready"...
[vm1] Waiting for SSH to become available...
[vm1] Machine is booted and ready for use!
...
notice: /Stage[main]/Java::Package_debian/Package[java]/ensure:
ensure changed 'purged' to 'present'
notice: Finished catalog run in 113.17 seconds
```

8. Check whether you are able to connect to the box and that JMeter was successfully installed on the machine:

```
vagrant ssh vm1
ls -l
```

   ° This should contain a `testplans` directory.

   ```
   ls -l /usr/local/
   ```

   ° This should contain some directories including a `jmeter` one.

Now our first VirtualBox is up and running, ready to execute our test plans.

Start up three additional console/shell windows, one for each additional virtual machine we will bring up. To bring up the second (vm2), third (vm3), and fourth (vm4) virtual machines, run the following commands, one in each of the new shell windows:

```
vagrant up vm2 --provider=aws
vagrant up vm3 --provider=aws
vagrant up vm4 --provider=aws
```

Verify each of them is properly set up, just like we did for the first virtual machine. With all four machines running, we are ready to proceed with executing our test plans.

# Executing the test plan

Since we are not using a master/slave node configuration in this section for reasons described earlier, we'll need to execute the following command on all four virtual machines simultaneously as best we can.

To execute our test plans, run the following on the virtual boxes:

On **vm1**, type (or copy) the following on the console:

```
/usr/local/jmeter/bin/jmeter -n -t testplans/browse-apple-itunes.jmx -l
vm1-out.csv
```

On **vm2**, type (or copy) the following on the console:

```
/usr/local/jmeter/bin/jmeter -n -t testplans/browse-apple-itunes.jmx -l
vm2-out.csv
```

On **vm3**, type (or copy) the following on the console:

```
/usr/local/jmeter/bin/jmeter -n -t testplans/browse-apple-itunes.jmx -l
vm3-out.csv
```

On **vm4**, type (or copy) the following on the console:

```
/usr/local/jmeter/bin/jmeter -n -t testplans/browse-apple-itunes.jmx -l
vm4-out.csv
```

These will run JMeter in a non-GUI mode and execute the `browse-apple-itunes.jmx` test plan. Each virtual machine will print simulation results to the CSV files. Therefore, **vm1** will output results to `vm1-out.csv`, **vm2** to `vm2-out.csv`, and so on.

Now that all the consoles are ready, press *Enter* on your keyboard in each console to execute the test plan on each virtual machine. You should see a log similar to each of the following on each console:

```
Created the tree successfully using testplans/browse-apple-itunes.jmx

Starting the test @ Fri Jan 23 20:49:38 UTC 2015 (1365108578406)

Waiting for possible shutdown message on port 4445

Generate Summary Results +    3592 in    82s =   43.9/s Avg:   1030 Min:
4 Max:   7299 Err:      0 (0.00%) Active: 208 Started: 300 Finished: 92

Generate Summary Results +    3008 in    55s =   54.8/s Avg:    541 Min:
4 Max:   6508 Err:      0 (0.00%) Active: 0 Started: 300 Finished: 300
```

```
Generate Summary Results =   6600 in    114s =   57.7/s Avg:    807 Min:
4 Max:   7299 Err:     0 (0.00%)

Tidying up ...    @ Fri Jan 23 20:51:34 UTC 2013 (1365108694177)

... end of run
```

The last line (... `end of run`) indicates that the test is finished on that node and the result is ready for viewing. You should be able to verify that the results file was generated by listing the contents of the current directory using the `ls -l` command. You should see an output of the `vmX-out.csv` format (where X will represent the node you are on. In our case, it's 1,2,3, or 4).

# Viewing the results from the virtual machines

To view the results, we need to grab the files off each host machine and then concatenate them together to form a composite whole. We can then view the final merged file using a JMeter GUI client. To grab the files, we can use any SFTP tool of our choice. If you are on a Unix-flavored machine, chances are that you already have the `scp` command-line utility handy. That is what we will be using here. To proceed, we will need the name of the host machine that we are trying to connect to. To get this, type the `exit` command on the console of the first virtual machine.

You will see a line similar to the following:

```
ubuntu@ip-10-190-237-149:~$ exit

logout

Connection to ec2-23-23-1-249.compute-1.amazonaws.com closed.
```

The `ec2-xxxxxx.compute-1.amazonaws.com` line is the host name of the machine. We can now connect to the box using our `keypair` file and retrieve the results file. At the console, issue the following command:

```
scp -i [PATH TO YOUR KEYPAIR FILE] ubuntu@[HOSTNAME]:"*.csv" [DESTINATION
DIRECTORY ON LOCAL MACHINE]
```

As an example, on our box, our `keypair` file named `book-test.pem` is stored under the `.ec2` directory in our home directory, and we want to place the results file in `/tmpdirectory`. Therefore, we run the following command:

```
scp -i ~/.ec2/book-test.pem ubuntu@ec2-23-23-1-249.compute-1.amazonaws.
com:"*.csv" /tmp
```

This will transfer all the `.csv` files on the AWS instance to our local machine under the `/tmp` directory.

Repeat the command for the three additional virtual boxes.

Remember to use the correct hostname for each VirtualBox.

After transferring all the result files from the virtual machines, we can terminate all the instances as we are done with them.

 AWS is a paid service, and you are charged per hour/per instance. If you are done with a box, remember to shut it down else you incur unnecessary charges.

You can either shut down each individually using `vagrant destroy [VM ALIAS NAME]` (`vagrant destroy vm1` will shut down virtual box aliased `vm1`), or shut all running instances down using `vagrant destroy`.

 You can always verify the state of your instances through the `vagrant status` command or through the AWS web console at `https://console.aws.amazon.com/ec2`.

With our entire results file from all hosts now available locally, we will need to merge them together to get an aggregate of response time across all hosts. We can do this with any editor that can deal with CSV file formats. Basically, you will open a file (say `vm1-out.csv`) and append the entire contents of the other files (`vm2-out.csv`, `vm3-out.csv`, and `vm4-out.csv`) to it. Alternatively, this can all be done from the command line. For those on unix-flavored machines, the `cat` command can be employed. Open the command line and change directory to the location where you have transferred the result files. Then run the following on the console:

```
cat vm1-out.csv vm2-out.csv vm3-out.csv vm4-out.csv >> merged-out.csv
```

 This assumes that you followed along with this section and named your result files from `vm1-out.csv` to `vm4-out.csv`, respectively.

This creates a file named `merged-out.csv` that can now be opened in our JMeter GUI client. To do that, perform the following steps:

1. Launch **JMeter** GUI.

2. Add a `Summary Report` listener by navigating to **Test Plan | Add | Listener | Summary Report**.

3. Click on **Summary Report**.

4. Click on the **Browse...** button.

5. Select the **merged-out.csv** file.

Since our test plan spins-off 300 users and runs for two iterations, each virtual node generates 600 samples. Since we ran this across four nodes, we have a total of 2,400 samples generated as can be seen from the Summary Report listener in the following screenshot:

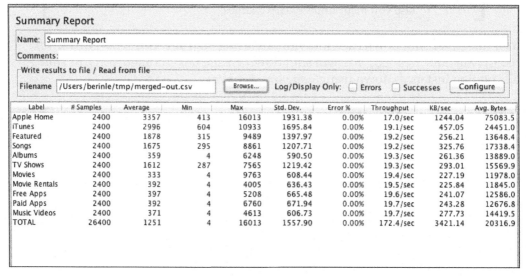

| Label | # Samples | Average | Min | Max | Std. Dev. | Error % | Throughput | KB/sec | Avg. Bytes |
|---|---|---|---|---|---|---|---|---|---|
| Apple Home | 2400 | 3357 | 413 | 16013 | 1931.38 | 0.00% | 17.0/sec | 1244.04 | 75083.5 |
| iTunes | 2400 | 2996 | 604 | 10933 | 1695.84 | 0.00% | 19.1/sec | 457.05 | 24451.0 |
| Featured | 2400 | 1878 | 315 | 9489 | 1397.97 | 0.00% | 19.2/sec | 256.21 | 13648.4 |
| Songs | 2400 | 1675 | 295 | 8861 | 1207.71 | 0.00% | 19.2/sec | 325.76 | 17338.4 |
| Albums | 2400 | 359 | 4 | 6248 | 590.50 | 0.00% | 19.3/sec | 261.36 | 13889.0 |
| TV Shows | 2400 | 1612 | 287 | 7565 | 1219.42 | 0.00% | 19.3/sec | 293.01 | 15569.9 |
| Movies | 2400 | 333 | 4 | 9763 | 608.44 | 0.00% | 19.4/sec | 227.19 | 11978.0 |
| Movie Rentals | 2400 | 392 | 4 | 4005 | 636.43 | 0.00% | 19.5/sec | 225.84 | 11845.0 |
| Free Apps | 2400 | 397 | 4 | 5208 | 665.48 | 0.00% | 19.6/sec | 241.07 | 12586.0 |
| Paid Apps | 2400 | 392 | 4 | 6760 | 671.94 | 0.00% | 19.7/sec | 243.28 | 12676.8 |
| Music Videos | 2400 | 371 | 4 | 4613 | 606.73 | 0.00% | 19.7/sec | 277.73 | 14419.5 |
| TOTAL | 26400 | 1251 | 4 | 16013 | 1557.90 | 0.00% | 172.4/sec | 3421.14 | 20316.9 |

Summary Report listener

We also see the Max response time is not too shabby. There were no errors reported on any of the nodes and the throughput was good for our run. These are not bad numbers considering we used AWS small instances. We can always put more stress on the application or web servers by spinning off more nodes to run test plans or using higher capacity machines on AWS. Although we have only used four virtual boxes for illustrative purposes here, nothing prevents you from scaling out to hundreds of machines to run your test plans. As you start to scale out to more and more servers for your test plans, it may become increasingly difficult and cumbersome to simultaneously start your test plans across all nodes.

At the time of this writing, we discovered yet another tool that promises to ease the management pain across multiple AWS nodes or inhouse networked machines. This tool helps spin off AWS instances (like we have done here), install JMeter, run a test plan distributing the load across the number of instances spun, and gather all the results from all hosts to your local box, all the while giving you the real-time aggregate information on the console. At the end of the tests, it terminates all AWS instances that were started. We gave it a spin, but couldn't quite get it working as advertised. It is still worth keeping an eye on the project, and you can find out more about it at `https://github.com/oliverlloyd/ jmeter-ec2`. Furthermore, we should mention that there are some services out on the web, helping to bring ease into distributed testing. Two of such services are Flood.io (`http://flood.io`) and BlazeMeter (`http://blazemeter.com/`). We will cover these two awesome cloud services in the sections that follow.

# Using cloud services

In the preceding section, we walked through how you can roll your own distributed testing infrastructure, if you desire or are constrained by something beyond your control. In this section, we discuss how you can take advantage of the existing cloud distributed testing services that aim to ease your overall setup and testing needs. They also help you perform your testing tasks more quickly and more efficiently. The two services discussed (Flood.io and BlazeMeter) take different approaches to tackling these problems, but ultimately you get similar results.

# Using Flood.io

Flood.io is described as a service that takes the pain out of setting up and maintaining cloud-based load and performance test infrastructure. It can be found at `http://flood.io`. With Flood.io, you upload an already recorded test script to its service and it takes care of the rest, ensuring that your tests are distributed among several machines while assembling important results and metrics in a beautiful and well-crafted UI, in real time as the test progresses.

Flood.io is a paid service, but you can register for a free user account at `http://flood.io` to follow along with the sample discussed here. The free user account gives you a monthly quota of an hour and allows you to run your tests for a maximum of five minutes after which it is shutdown. This will give you a taste of how nice this cloud service is.

> Download the entire code sample for the book at `https://github.com/ptwj/ptwj-code/archive/master.zip`. You'll find the files needed for this section in the `chap6` directory.

Rather than discussing it, let's take out a prerecorded test script (`chap6/railway.jmx`) and take it for a spin on its service:

1.  Register for a free account at `http://flood.io`.
2.  Log in to your account.
3.  Once logged in, click on the **Create Flood** button.
4.  Drag and drop the simulation file (`railway.jmx`) that we will be using for our test into the **Upload Files** box.
5.  In addition, drag and drop the supporting data files (`cars.txt`, `trains.txt`, and `stations.txt`) for the test into the **Upload Files** box.
6.  Optionally, you can provide a name for your flood in the **Name** textbox.
7.  In the **Grids** dropdown, select the only available grid on the free tier.
8.  Optionally, you can enter the number of threads, ramp up, and duration into their respective boxes, but for our purposes, you can skip them.
9.  Click on the **Start Flood** button.

Momentarily, your test simulation (what Flood.io refers as a flood) will be started
and live results will be displayed on the screen once the test has enough information
to display meaningful reports. The actual simulation run for this section can be seen
at `http://bit.ly/1Ejpnji`. The following is the result of our test run on Flood.io.

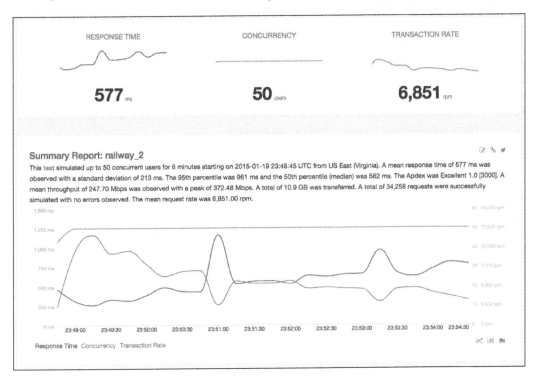

In addition to providing easy setup of distributed testing, it is worth noting that
Flood.io provides some useful features such as:

- Allowing you to easily emulate various network topologies, for example,
  mobile, broadband, and so on.
- Allowing you to override JMeter parameters in your test plans
- Allowing you to override the URL parameters for your test plans
- Scheduling tests to kick-off at a later point in the future
- Providing a ruby gem that allows you write test plans in an expressive
  domain specific language (DSL)
- Allowing you launch tests on its cloud infrastructure without opening
  a browser

All in all, Flood.io is an excellent cloud testing service to consider if your budget permits. Next, we explore BlazeMeter, another good cloud testing service.

# Using BlazeMeter

BlazeMeter is a cloud testing service that describes itself as the load testing cloud. It is aimed at getting you up and running with distributed testing in no time. Their platform allows you to test and monitor mobile and web applications under heavy and realistic loads while presenting you with useful metrics and reports. It is a paid service, but they do offer a free account that we will be using for the purpose of this section. The free account allows you to simulate at most 50 users for a maximum of 1 hour, which is sufficient to get a feel of the service.

> Download the entire code sample for the book at https://github. com/ptwj/ptwj-code/archive/master.zip. You'll find the files needed for this section in the chap6 directory.

Let's jump right in and use the same sample as we did in the preceding exercise:

1. Register for a free account at http://blazemeter.com/.
2. Log in to your account.
3. Once logged in, click on the **Add Test** button on the top navigation bar.
4. Provide a name for your test in the **Test Name** textbox.
5. In the **Load Origin location** dropdown, you can optionally switch to a different region, but BlazeMeter is smart enough to default to the closest region to your geographical location.
6. Click on the **Upload Files** button and select the simulation file (railway.jmx) and the three supporting data files (cars.txt, trains.txt, and stations.txt) for our tests.
7. Adjust the ramp up time from the default of 300 seconds to 10 seconds by moving the slider down as needed.
8. Reduce the test duration from the default of 50 minutes to 10 minutes by moving the slider down as needed.

9. In the **JMeter Version** dropdown, select **2.12 BlazeMeter**.

10. Leave the rest of the values unchanged.

11. Click on the **Save** button.

12. Once saved, BlazeMeter gives you a preview of test settings allowing you to make additional modifications to it as you desire.

13. Once you are satisfied, click on the **Start** button to begin the test simulation.

14. Another dialog box pops up letting you know your test will terminate after 1 hour and requires you to acknowledge that you are authorized to run the test. Click on the **Launch Server** button.

15. The test simulation will then begin, and real-time reports can be seen by clicking on the **Report** tab in the top navigation bar. In addition, an e-mail will be sent to you once the test has completed, which is pretty cool!

The real-time graph allows you to view different matrices regarding your tests including active and max users, response time, latency, hits per second, throughput per second (KB/s), errors, and so on. In the **Load Results** tab, you also get a familiar table view (similar to what you see in the Aggregate Report Listener) of your results.

In the **Waterfall** tab, you get yet another view of metrics data to analyze your test results. These include page load and a detailed breakdown of each request and where time was spent.

In the **Monitoring** tab, you get a view of the system metrics as your test was being conducted. These include CPU, Memory, Network I/O, and Connections. These are all useful analytic metrics that can help you identify and pinpoint performance bottlenecks in the application under test. The last tab, **Logs**, give the public IP addresses of the machines that were used to conduct your tests and access to the Jmeter console logs generated during your test run which you can download and further analyze.

Our run at the time of writing can be reached at `https://a.blazemeter.com/report/r-ec254c21d52f30f1`.

In addition to these, BlazeMeter offers even more useful features including:

- Allowing you to easily emulate various network topologies for example, mobile, broadband, and so on
- Allowing you to override JMeter parameters in your test plans
- Allowing you to override the URL parameters for your test plans
- Scheduling tests to kick-off at a later point in the future
- Integration with New Relic (`http://newrelic.com`) allows your valuable insight into application metrics as your tests is being conducted
- Integration with Amazon's AWS CloudWatch to monitor your resources on AWS if the application under test happens to be housed there
- User experience monitoring with Selenium (`http://docs.seleniumhq.org/`)

BlazeMeter is an exceptional cloud testing service to consider if your budget permits.

So with that, we wrap up our look into distributed testing with JMeter. Though the test plan we used had no input test data, nothing prevents you from using one that does. Also, all the other techniques we learned in other chapters can be applied whenever they make sense. And not using a master/node configuration got us past the hurdle of known limitations with that approach. These include:

- Network saturation due to high number of slave nodes writing to the master node

- RMI communication is not possible across subnets without a proxy thereby forcing slaves and the master to be on the same subnet, in these cases

- The master node server can be easily overwhelmed with very few slave nodes reporting to it, depending on its resources (CPU and memory)

# Summary

We covered quite a lot of ground in this chapter. We learned how we can distribute a load using different techniques when executing test plans. We learned how to have JMeter work in a master/node configuration. With the help of tools such as Vagrant, we made a daunting task really easy. We learned how to spin-off several node machines on the same physical box (or different boxes) and use a master node to control them all from a JMeter GUI. While convenient, we saw that this method was limiting in terms of scalability. As the number of slave nodes grew, the master quickly became the bottleneck due to high I/O generated from several nodes trying to report progress to it. To overcome such restrictions and ultimately achieve infinite scalability, we learned how to run several test machines in parallel to execute our test plans. In the process, we leveraged the AWS infrastructure and saw how we can use the cloud to aid more efficient testing, thereby helping us reach our goals.

In the last sections, we covered two outstanding cloud services Flood.io and BlazeMeter and saw how they take the pain out of distributed testing while still providing all the useful features needed for testing and monitoring.

In the next chapter, we will look at some tips that are helpful and handy when working with JMeter such as JMeter Properties and Variables, JMeter Functions and Regular Expression Tester, to name a few.

# 7
# Helpful Tips

At this point, you have hopefully become familiar with the inner workings of JMeter and are comfortable with using it to achieve most of your testing needs. However, before we wrap up the book, there are some helpful tips worth mentioning that will make working with JMeter more pleasant and perhaps save you time in the process. These are some techniques we learned over the years, and they have proven to be useful in almost every environment we've found ourselves in.

## JMeter properties and variables

JMeter properties are defined in `jmeter.properties` (located in the `$JMETER_HOME/bin` directory), which is global in nature and used to define some defaults JMeter uses. The value of the `remote_hosts` property encountered in the previous chapter is a good example of this. Properties can be referenced from within a test plan, but cannot be used for thread-specific values because of their global nature (shared among all threads).

JMeter variables, on the other hand, are local to each thread. The values may stay the same or vary between threads. In cases where a variable is updated by a thread, only the thread copy of the variable is changed, thus remaining invisible to other running threads. A good example of this is the Regular Expression Extractor post processor that we encountered in the previous chapters. The values extracted and acted upon are in the context of the samples of the running thread. The variables that are extracted are user-defined and available to the whole test plan at the startup. If the same variable is defined by multiple user-defined variable elements, the last one wins.

As simple as they appear, using JMeter variables wisely can help save your time by allowing you to use the same recorded scripts from one environment to another environment without having to rescript for every single environment you are targeting, provided the two environments are structured similarly architecturally. For instance, test plans recorded against the **User Acceptance Test (UAT)** environment can be run in production if these two environments bear a resemblance in structure. To accomplish that, you can either define **User Defined Variables (UDV)** at the test plan root level, or replace individual URLs for HTTP Request samplers. For example, we can define the following UDVs at the test plan root level:

| | |
|---|---|
| `app_url` | `${__P(app_url, https://uat.fastcompany.com/someapp)}` |
| `sso_url` | `${__P(sso_url, https://sso.uat.fastcompany.com/login)}` |
| `threads` | `${__P(threads, 10)}` |
| `loops` | `${__P(loops, 30)}` |

With such a configuration, we defined default values for `app_url`, `sso_url`, `threads`, and `loops` and still provided the ability to override them from the command line as follows:

```
jmeter ... -Japp_url=https://fastcompany.com/someapp Jsso_url=https://
sso.fastcompany.com/login -Jloops=15
```

This will make our test plans use an `app_url` variable having the value `https://fastcompany.com/someapp`, the `sso_url` variable having the value `https://sso.fastcompany.com/login`, and the `loops` variable having the value `15`. The number of threads will remain `10` (by default) since it wasn't overridden. This concept saves a lot of time when developing test plans against various environments, allowing you to record once and target various environments with the same set of scripts. For instance, this is useful when a particular environment isn't ready yet and scripts have already been developed targeting an active environment. Once the environment becomes available, the same scripts can target the newly available environment without having to rerecord them.

We bundled a sample with the book (`exilys-bank-scenario-3.jmx`). It's from the banking application sample test plan that we saw in *Chapter 2, Recording Your First Test* . It is hosted on two different cloud providers: OpenShift at `http://exilysbank-berinle.rhcloud.com` and AppFog at `http://exilysbank.aws.af.cm`. It runs against AppFog by default. To run it against OpenShift, you will need to override the hostname variable when you start JMeter like the following:

```
jmeter -Jhostname=exilysbank-berinle.rhcloud.com
```

# JMeter functions

JMeter functions are special values that can populate fields or any sampler or other element in the test plan. They take the following form:

```
${__functionName(var1,var2,var3)}
```

Here, `__functionName` matches any of the many function names JMeter offers. Parentheses surround the parameters sent to the function, which can vary from function to function. Functions with no parameters don't need the parentheses, for example, `${__threadNum}`. A list of all available functions can be found on JMeter's website at `http://jmeter.apache.org/usermanual/functions.html`. Functions are divided into seven main categories. They are given here along with their examples:

- **Information**: `threadNum`, `machineIP`, `time`, and so on
- **Input**: `CSVRead`, `XPath`, and so on
- **Calculation**: `counter`, `Random`, `UUID`, and so on
- **Scripting**: `javaScript`, `BeanShell`, and so on
- **Properties**: `property`, `P`, `setProperty`, and so on
- **Variables**: `split`, `eval`, and so on
- **String**: `char`, `unescape`, and so on

Functions can prove useful in certain situations, allowing the computation of new values at a runtime based on previous response data, such as which thread the function is in, time, and numerous other sources. Their values are generated afresh for every request throughout the course of the test. There are also some restrictions regarding where certain functions can be invoked. Since JMeter thread variables are not fully initialized when functions are processed, variable names passed as parameters will not be set up. This causes variable references to not work.

Functions are shared between threads in the test plan. Each occurrence of a function call is handled by a separate function instance.

# The Regular Expression tester

Throughout the course of the book, we have seen Regular Expression Extractor post processors in action in several of our scenarios. These components allow you to extract values from a server response using a Perl-type regular expression. As a post processor, this element executes after each sample request in its scope, applying the regular expression; extracts the requested values, generating the template string; and finally stores the result into a given variable name, which can then be referenced further down the test plan. To fully maximize the use of the Regular Expression Extractor post processor, you should get acquainted with regular expressions in general. There are numerous online resources that can help, but you can start with this one: `http://www.regular-expressions.info/tutorial.html`. The **RegExp Tester** view is one of the options that you can choose from the **View Results Tree** listener drop-down menu. It allows you to test various regular expressions against the server response on a per-sampler basis. When you are interested in extracting a variable or group of variables that vary dynamically based on which thread is currently executing, this gives you the maximum flexibility to test and tune your regular expression till you find the exact match that suits your needs. Without such an element, ample time can be spent nailing down the right pattern matcher, as it will involve rerunning your test plan several times with various inaccurate expressions, hoping it eventually matches:

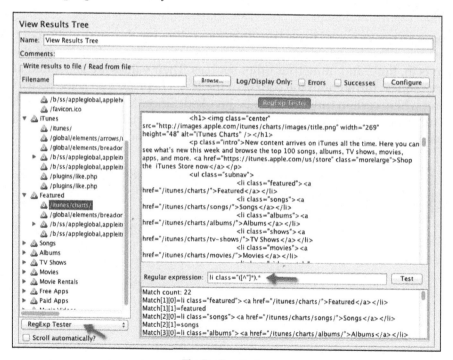

The RegExp Tester

In our browse iTunes store test plan from the previous chapter, say we were interested in extracting the `class` elements from the HTML response of the `/itunes/charts/` sampler. Once the test has been exercised, we can explore the **RegExp Tester** view to find the right regular expression for this. For our purpose, it came down to `li class="([^"]*).*`, which matched 22 elements, listed in the bottom half of the window as seen in the previous screenshot. We can then copy that pattern into a Regular Expression Extractor post processor under the `/itunes/charts/` sampler and store the results in a variable to use further down the chain in our test plan.

# The debug sampler

The debug sampler generates a sample containing all the values of JMeter variables and/or properties. A **View Results Tree** listener must be present in the test plan to view its results. This nifty component helps you debug your test plans appropriately, providing you with the tools to analyze the runtime-assigned values of various variables during test execution. In our aforementioned example, suppose we add a **Regular Expression Extractor** post processor to the `/itunes/charts` sampler and store it in a variable, we will be able to view the value assigned to the variable, and more importantly how to get to the different values if there is more than one match. To add a **Debug** Sampler, right-click on **Thread Group**, and navigate to **Add | Sampler | Debug Sampler**, as follows:

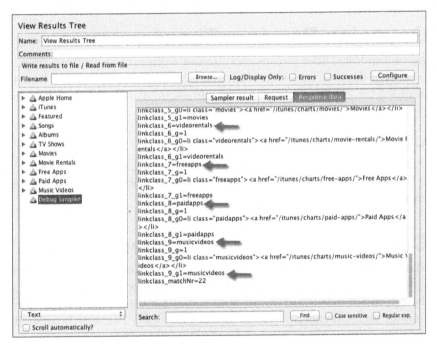

The debug sampler via the View Result Listener

As you can see from this screenshot, the multiple matches are stored under `linkclass_n` (where n is a match position), followed by the variable name declared in our Regular Expression Extractor post processor. Thus, we can get hold of the first match as `linkclass_1`, the second as `linkclass_2`, and so on. As you record more and more complex scripts, you will find the debug sampler to be an invaluable component that is worth keeping handy.

# Using timers in your test plan

By default, JMeter doesn't put timers in your test plans when a scenario is recorded. This is far from reality. Ideally, users will have a think or wait time between page views and requests. Getting JMeter to simulate such pauses or waits makes your test plans more realistic, bringing it closer to how actual users may behave. JMeter offers various built-in timer components that help achieve this. Each varies from the others in how it varies the simulated pauses. The following is a list of some of the included timers at the time of writing of this book.

## The Constant Timer

The Constant Timer is used if you want each thread to pause for the same amount of time between requests.

## The Gaussian Random Timer

The Gaussian Random Timer pauses each thread request for a random amount of time with most of the time intervals occurring near a particular value. The total delay is the sum of the Gaussian distributed value times, the value specified, and the offset.

## The Uniform Random Timer

The Uniform Random Timer pauses thread requests for a random amount of time, with each time interval having the same probability of occurring. The total delay is the sum of the random and offset values.

## The Constant Throughput Timer

The Constant Throughput Timer introduces variable pauses calculated to keep the total throughput, that is, samples per minute as close as possible to the targeted figure. Though called a constant throughput timer, the throughput can be varied by using a counter value, JavaScript value, BeanShell value, or remote BeanShell server.

# The Synchronizing Timer

The Synchronizing Timer helps simulate large instantaneous loads on various points in the test plan by blocking threads until a certain number of threads have been blocked and then released all at once.

# The Poisson Random Timer

The Poisson Random Timer, like the Gaussian Random Timer, pauses thread requests for a random amount of time, with most of the time intervals occurring near a particular value. The total delay is the sum of the Poisson distributed value and the offset value.

Any of these timers can be added by right-clicking on a thread group and navigating to **Add | Timer | (Timer to Add)**. You can read more about each of these timers and more at JMeter's website at http://jmeter.apache.org/usermanual/component_reference.html#timers.

# The JDBC Request sampler

Sometimes, it's necessary to test durability and I/O operations against the database directly. How fast are insert, update, and select queries on the tables in question? For such tests, JMeter provides a JDBC Request sampler to help issue SQL queries against the database. However, to use it, we need to set up a JDBC Connection Configuration component. Setting up this component requires us to point to a database. Therefore, let's go ahead and set up the database. Normally, this will already be set up for you to test against, but for illustrative purposes, we are going to assume that none has been set up. We will be using H2, an open source, pure Java SQL database. It is lightweight and relatively easy to set up. You can find more details about H2 at http://www.h2database.com/html/main.html.

# Setting up the H2 database

To set up the H2 database, do the following:

1. Download a distribution from http://www.h2database.com/html/download.html.
2. Extract the archive to a location of your choice. We will refer to this as H2_HOME.
3. From the command line, go to the H2_HOME/bin folder.

4. Start the H2 database server by issuing either of these commands.

   ° On Unix:

   ```
   ./h2.sh
   ```

   ° On Windows:

   ```
   h2.bat
   ```

5. This will launch your browser and point to the H2 Admin console, as seen in the following screenshot:

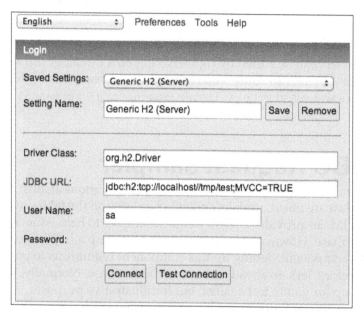

The H2 Admin console (before the connection)

6. Create a test database named `test` by changing your **JDBC URL** value to either of the following:

   ° On Unix:

   ```
   jdbc:h2:tcp://localhost//tmp/test;MVCC=TRUE
   ```

   ° On Windows:

   ```
   jdbc:h2:tcp://localhost/c:/test;MVCC=TRUE
   ```

7. Click on the **Connect** button.

8. Create the sample table that we will be using to test by copying the following script into the space provided in the console (see the screenshot that follows the next screenshot):

```
DROP TABLE IF EXISTS TEST;
CREATE TABLE TEST(ID INT PRIMARY KEY, NAME VARCHAR(255));
INSERT INTO TEST VALUES(1, 'Hello');
INSERT INTO TEST VALUES(2, 'World');
```

9. Click on the **Run** button.

Now that we have a database and table to test with, we can go ahead and configure a **JDBC Connection Configuration** component to point to it.

 Since H2 is Java-based, to run it, you need to have a JRE (Java Runtime Environment) set up on the machine of choice. Please refer to *Chapter 1, Performance Testing Fundamentals,* for instructions on setting up JRE on your machine if you don't already have it.

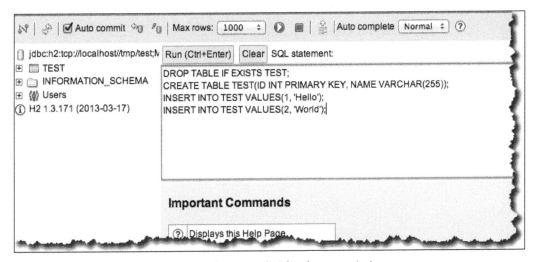

The H2 Admin console (after the connection)

# Configuring a JDBC Connection Configuration component

As the name suggests, this component helps create a connection to the database from the supplied settings. Each thread can get its own dedicated connection or connections may be pooled between threads.

1.  Copy the JDBC driver (`h2-1.3.171.jar` or similar) from the `H2_HOME/bin` folder to the `JMETER_HOME/lib/ext` folder.

2.  Add a **JDBC Connection Configuration** component to the test plan by right-clicking on **Test Plan** and navigating to **Test Plan | Add | Config Element | JDBC Connection Configuration**.

3.  Configure the properties as follows:
    - **Variable Name**: `testPool`
    - **Validation Query**: `Select 1 from dual`
    - **Database URL**: `jdbc:h2:tcp://localhost//tmp/test;MVCC=TRUE` (those using Windows should use `jdbc:h2:tcp://localhost/c:/test;MVCC=TRUE`)
    - **JDBC Driver class**: `org.h2.Driver`
    - **Username**: `sa`

4.  Leave the rest of the configurations as they are:

## JDBC Connection Configuration

Name: JDBC Connection Configuration

Comments:

**Variable Name Bound to Pool**

Variable Name: testPool

**Connection Pool Configuration**

Max Number of Connections: 10

Pool Timeout: 10000

Idle Cleanup Interval (ms): 60000

Auto Commit: True

Transaction Isolation: DEFAULT

**Connection Validation by Pool**

Keep–Alive: True

Max Connection age (ms): 5000

Validation Query: Select 1 from dual

**Database Connection Configuration**

Database URL: jdbc:h2:tcp://localhost//tmp/test;MVCC=TRUE

JDBC Driver class: org.h2.Driver

Username: sa

Password:

The JDBC Connection Configuration component

# Adding a JDBC Request sampler

Now that we have a **JDBC Connection Configuration** component configured, the final step is to add a **JDBC Request** sampler to our test plan to make use of it. Adding that is not different from how we added other samplers throughout the book:

1. Create a **Thread Group** element, if none already exist, by right-clicking on **Test Plan** and navigating to **Test Plan** | **Threads** | **Thread Group**.

2. Add a **JDBC Request** sampler by right-clicking on **Thread Group** and navigating to **Thread Group** | **Add** | **Sampler** | **JDBC Request**.

3. In the SQL Query input field, type in the following:

   `SELECT * FROM TEST`

4. Add a View Results Tree listener by right-clicking on **Thread Group** and navigating to **Add | Listener | View Results Tree**.

5. Save the test plan.

6. Execute the test.

Although a simple query, it illustrates the concept. The **JDBC Request** sampler allows you to issue complex queries with bind parameters, inserts, updates, deletes, and even stored procedures. More details can be found at `http://jmeter.apache.org/usermanual/build-db-test-plan.html` and `http://jmeter.apache.org/usermanual/component_reference.html#JDBC_Request`.

# Using a MongoDB Sampler

In the previous section, we saw how JMeter can be used to directly test a relational database. A new category of databases termed NoSQL (Not Only SQL or No SQL) are on the rise and it is not uncommon to come across applications using these databases either in combination with relational ones, or entirely as the only database. These databases offer certain features such as document-oriented storage, schema-less, high availability, sharding, map/reduce, and so on that make them more attractive than their relational counterparts for certain use cases. You can read more about NoSQL databases at `https://en.wikipedia.org/wiki/NoSQL`.

The popular NoSQL databases are MongoDB, Couchbase, Redis, Apache Cassandra, Riak, Amazon DynamoDB, to name a few.

Since MongoDB is one of the most popular ones, JMeter comes bundled with components that can help you directly test MongoDB databases with no additional plugins. This can come in handy if you would like to test the database isolated from the interfacing application using it.

To test MongoDB with JMeter, do the following:

1. Install MongoDB as described in the online documentations at `http://docs.mongodb.org/manual/installation/`

> For easier use, make sure `MONGODB_HOME/bin` is available at your path, so you can access commands such as mongod and mongo easily from any terminal and/or directory.

2. Start the MongoDB instance by opening a terminal window and typing `mongod`.

3. If your installation was successful and `mongod` correctly exists in your PATH, then you should see something similar to the following screenshot:

```
→  ~  mongod                                                    berinle@bayo-imac
2015-03-09T11:45:23.276-0400 I CONTROL  [initandlisten] MongoDB starting : pid=41194 port=27017 dbpath=/us
r/local/var/mongodb 64-bit host=bayo-imac
2015-03-09T11:45:23.277-0400 I CONTROL  [initandlisten] db version v3.0.0
2015-03-09T11:45:23.277-0400 I CONTROL  [initandlisten] git version: nogitversion
2015-03-09T11:45:23.277-0400 I CONTROL  [initandlisten] build info: Darwin miniyosemite.local 14.1.0 Darwi
n Kernel Version 14.1.0: Mon Dec 22 23:10:38 PST 2014; root:xnu-2782.10.72~2/RELEASE_X86_64 x86_64 BOOST_L
IB_VERSION=1_49
2015-03-09T11:45:23.277-0400 I CONTROL  [initandlisten] allocator: system
2015-03-09T11:45:23.277-0400 I CONTROL  [initandlisten] options: { storage: { dbPath: "/usr/local/var/mong
odb" } }
2015-03-09T11:45:23.317-0400 I JOURNAL  [initandlisten] journal dir=/usr/local/var/mongodb/journal
2015-03-09T11:45:23.317-0400 I JOURNAL  [initandlisten] recover : no journal files present, no recovery ne
eded
2015-03-09T11:45:23.337-0400 I JOURNAL  [durability] Durability thread started
2015-03-09T11:45:23.338-0400 I JOURNAL  [journal writer] Journal writer thread started
2015-03-09T11:45:24.512-0400 I NETWORK  [initandlisten] waiting for connections on port 27017

[1]                          1:mongod*                        "bayo-imac" 11:45 09-Mar-15
```

Starting mongodb instance using mongod command

4. Launch JMeter.

5. Add Thread Group by navigating to **Test Plan | Add | Threads(Users) | Thread Group**.

6. Add the **MongoDB Source Config** element by navigating to **Thread Group | Add | Config Element | MongoDB Source Config**.

7. Fill in the contents as follows:

   ○ Server Address List: `127.0.0.1`

   ○ MongoDB Source: `mongo`

8. Add the MongoDB Script component to the Thread Group by navigating to **Thread Group | Add | Sampler | MongoDB Script**.

9. Fill in the following details:

   ○ **MongoDB Source**: `mongo` (should match the name specified in step 7)

   ○ **Database Name**: `ptwj`

   ○ **Username**: (leave it blank)

- ○ **Password**: (leave it blank)
- ○ **The script to run**: Copy the contents of `https://raw.githubusercontent.com/ptwj/ptwj-code/master/chap7/ch7_mongo_script.txt` and paste into the text area

 Any valid mongo script can be filled in the script to run text area, depending on your testing needs. Here, we are just testing inserts. The script we run is bundled with the sample code under the `ch7_mongo_script.txt` name. It can also be found here `https://raw.githubusercontent.com/ptwj/ptwj-code/master/chap7/ch7_mongo_script.txt`.

10. Add a **View Results Tree** listener to your test plan (**Test plan | Add | Listener | View Results Tree**).

11. Save and run the test plan. Observe the results of the execution.

12. The Response tab of the View Results Tree component should report ok indicating that the script is successfully completed.

13. You can verify that the entries successfully made it into the targeted mongo collection by doing the following from the terminal (in sequence):

```
mongo
use ptwj
db.posts.count()
db.posts.find()
```

The `mongo` command opens up a client connection to the MongoDB server. The `use ptwj` command instructs MongoDB if we want to switch to the `ptwj` database. This matches the database name that we specified in Step 9. The `db.posts.count()` counts the number of records we have in the posts collection. The last command, `db.posts.find()` prints all the contents we have in the posts collection.

For additional information on MongoDB, please refer to this link: `http://www.mongodb.org/`.

# A Dummy Sampler

Though not part of the built-in JMeter samplers, this sampler can be added to your JMeter toolkit via the JMeter extensions project. We discussed this in detail in *Chapter 5, Resource Monitoring*, so if you don't already have it configured, please refer to the chapter to get the gist of it. This sampler generates samples with just the values that are defined for it. It comes in extremely handy when debugging post processors without having to repeat the entire execution of the test plan or waiting for the exact condition in the application under testing.

This component allows you to determine if the response should be marked a successful sample, what response code to return, the response message, the latency, and response times. In addition, it allows you to specify a request and a response, which can be anything you choose; for example, HTML, XML, and JSON.

Once the plugins have been properly installed into your JMeter instance, you should see additional samplers available to pick from:

1.  Add a **Thread Group** element to the test plan by right-clicking on **Test Plan** and navigating to **Threads | Thread Group**.

2.  Add a **Dummy Sampler** element by right-clicking on **Thread Group** and navigating to **Add | Sampler | jp@gc - Dummy Sampler**. For the contents of the Response Data, add the following HTML snippet:

```
<html>
<head>
  <title>Welcome to Debug Sampler</title>
</head>
<body>
  This is a test
</body>
</html>
```

3.  Add a **View Results Tree** listener by right-clicking on **Thread Group** and navigating to **Add | Listener | View Results Tree**.

4.  Save the test plan.

5. Execute the test:

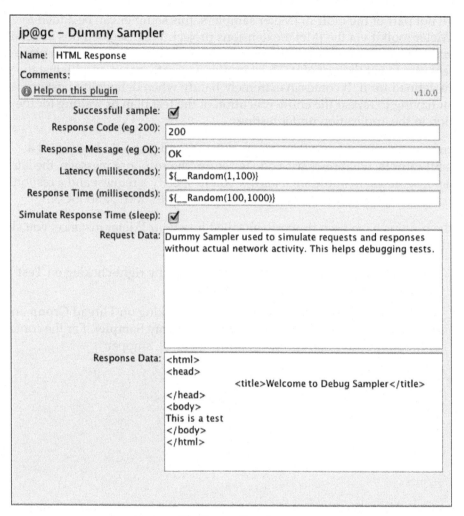

The Dummy Sampler

See the bundled `dummy-sampler.jmx` file for the full example.

# The JSON Path Extractor element

Another helpful nugget in the JMeter plugin's project is the JSON Path Extractor element. This makes working with JSON pure bliss. It helps extract data out of a JSON response using JSONPath syntax (`http://goessner.net/articles/JsonPath/index.html#e2`). For complex JSON structures, using JMeter's bundled XPath Extractor can sometimes lead to heartache when trying to get at targeted elements. Where XPath Extractor fails, JSON Path Extractor shines.

Consider a JSON structure like the following:

```
{ "store": {
    "book": [
{ "category": "reference",
        "author": "Nigel Rees",
        "title": "Sayings of the Century",
        "price": 8.95
      },
{ "category": "fiction",
        "author": "Evelyn Waugh",
        "title": "Sword of Honour",
        "price": 12.99
      },
{ "category": "fiction",
        "author": "Herman Melville",
        "title": "Moby Dick",
        "isbn": "0-553-21311-3",
        "price": 8.99
      },
{ "category": "fiction",
        "author": "J. R. R. Tolkien",
        "title": "The Lord of the Rings",
        "isbn": "0-395-19395-8",
        "price": 22.99
      }
    ],
    "bicycle": {
      "color": "red",
      "price": 19.95
    }
  }
}
```

If you wanted to get to the title of the second book in the store, an expression like `$.store.book[1].title` gets you there swiftly. No matter how nested the structure is, JSON Path Extractor gets the job done elegantly. See the two examples that accomplish this in this book: `JSONPathExtractorExample.jmx` (from the JMeter plugin's site) and `dummy-sampler.jmx`.

# Handling RESTful web services

An increasing number of applications are shifting to RESTful web services due to their simplicity to build, test, and consume compared to their SOAP counterparts. All REST communication is done over the HTTP protocol between the parties involved. HTTP is used for CRUD (create, read, update, and delete) operations. The built-in **HTTP Request** sampler in JMeter is more than up to the task. It supports GET, POST, PUT, and DELETE operations, among other things. The body of the request can be in XML or JSON format. An HTTP Header Manager component can be used to send additional HTTP header attributes if needed.

In our sample, we are going to create a new person in our sample application using a POST request, and then verify that the person was actually created using a GET request:

1. Create a new test plan.

2. Add a new **Thread Group** (by navigating to **Test Plan | Add | Thread Group**).

3. Add an **HTTP Request** sampler (this retrieves all the people records in our application so far), by navigating to **Thread Group | Add | Sampler | HTTP Request**. Call it `Get All People`. You will get the following fields. Fill in their values as given here:
    - **Server Name:** `jmeterbook.aws.af.cm`
    - **Method:** GET
    - **Path:** `/person/list`

4. Add another **HTTP Request** sampler by navigating to **Thread Group | Add | Sampler | HTTP Request** (this will create a new person record). Call it `Save Person()`.
    - **Server Name:** `jmeterbook.aws.af.cm`
    - **Method:** POST
    - **Post Body:** `{"firstName":"Test", "lastName":"Jmeter", "jobs":[{"id":5}]}`

5. Add a **JSON Path Extractor** element as a child element of the `Save Person` sampler.

   ○ **Name**: `person_id`

   ○ **JSON path**: `$.id`

6. Add another **HTTP Request** sampler (this will retrieve the newly created person using the extracted ID). Call it `Get Person`.

   ○ **Server Name**: `jmeterbook.aws.af.cm`

   ○ **Method**: `GET`

   ○ **Path**: `/person/get/${person_id}`

7. Add a **View Results Tree** listener.

8. Save the test plan.

9. Execute the test plan.

If all was correctly done, a new person with the name **Test JMeter** will be created in our application, and you can verify this by pointing your browser to `http://jmeterbook.aws.af.cm/person/list`. By the same token, we can issue `DELETE` and `PUT` requests to delete and update resources if our application supports it.

# Summary

In this chapter, we learned some helpful tips that are essential for making testing with JMeter more pleasurable. We covered variables, functions, regular expression testers, and timers, to name a few. Along the way, we covered some additional helpful components provided by the excellent JMeter plugin extensions. We barely scratched the surface of the additional components it provides. We looked at JSON Extractor and Dummy Sampler to name just a few. For a full list of all components, we encourage you to read up on their website at `https://code.google.com/p/jmeter-plugins/`. Finally, we looked at how JMeter can help us work with the database and REST web services.

We hope by now that you know enough about JMeter to become proficient and attain your testing goals. In just a short time, you have grown from novice to pro. Though we can't cover all JMeter has to offer, we hope that we covered enough to make you see it as a valuable tool of choice when embarking on your next performance testing engagement and that you enjoyed reading the book as much as we enjoyed writing it.

# Index

command-line options 14, 15
in non-GUI mode 16, 17
in server mode 17
proxy server, configuring 15, 16
scripts 13, 14

**JMeter slave nodes**
Apple iTunes, URL 98
configuring 91, 92
master node, configuring 95-102
multiple slave nodes, configuring on
single box 99-101
one slave per machine, configuring 92-95
one slave per machine, URL 92

**JMeter test, anatomy**
about 39
assertions 43
configuration elements 43
controllers 41
listeners 42
logic controllers 42
postprocessor elements 43
preprocessor elements 43
samplers 41
test fragments 42
test plan 40
thread groups 40
timers 43

**JSON**
URL 49

**JSON data**
BSF Postprocessor, using 55-57
posting 49-53
reading 53, 54

**JSON Path Extractor element**
about 135, 136
URL 135

# L

listeners **42**
load testing **8**
logic controllers **42**

# M

machine system settings
changing 25-27

master 89
**MongoDB sampler**
testing, with JMeter 130-132
URL 130-132
using 130-132
**mongo script**
URL 132
**monitor listeners**
adding, to test plan 83-86

# N

**New Relic**
URL 116
**non-GUI mode, JMeter**
running in 16, 17
**NoSQL databases**
URL 130

# O

**OpenShift**
URL 120

# P

**performance testing**
about 3-7
and tuning 7
baselines 8
load testing 8
**Poisson Random Timer 125**
**postprocessor elements 43**
**preprocessor elements 43**
**proxy server**
configuring 15, 16

# R

**radio buttons**
handling 47
URL 47
**radio group**
URL 47
**regular expression**
URL 38
**Regular Expression Extractor component**
configuration variables 38, 39

# Thank you for buying
# Performance Testing with JMeter
## *Second Edition*

## About Packt Publishing

Packt, pronounced 'packed', published its first book, *Mastering phpMyAdmin for Effective MySQL Management*, in April 2004, and subsequently continued to specialize in publishing highly focused books on specific technologies and solutions.

Our books and publications share the experiences of your fellow IT professionals in adapting and customizing today's systems, applications, and frameworks. Our solution-based books give you the knowledge and power to customize the software and technologies you're using to get the job done. Packt books are more specific and less general than the IT books you have seen in the past. Our unique business model allows us to bring you more focused information, giving you more of what you need to know, and less of what you don't.

Packt is a modern yet unique publishing company that focuses on producing quality, cutting-edge books for communities of developers, administrators, and newbies alike. For more information, please visit our website at www.packtpub.com.

## About Packt Open Source

In 2010, Packt launched two new brands, Packt Open Source and Packt Enterprise, in order to continue its focus on specialization. This book is part of the Packt Open Source brand, home to books published on software built around open source licenses, and offering information to anybody from advanced developers to budding web designers. The Open Source brand also runs Packt's Open Source Royalty Scheme, by which Packt gives a royalty to each open source project about whose software a book is sold.

## Writing for Packt

We welcome all inquiries from people who are interested in authoring. Book proposals should be sent to author@packtpub.com. If your book idea is still at an early stage and you would like to discuss it first before writing a formal book proposal, then please contact us; one of our commissioning editors will get in touch with you.

We're not just looking for published authors; if you have strong technical skills but no writing experience, our experienced editors can help you develop a writing career, or simply get some additional reward for your expertise.

## Performance Testing with JMeter 2.9

ISBN: 978-1-78216-584-2        Paperback: 148 pages

Learn how to test web applications using Apache JMeter with practical, hands-on examples

1. Create realistic and maintainable scripts for web applications.

2. Use various JMeter components to achieve testing goals.

3. Removal of unnecessary errors and code compilation.

4. Acquire skills that will enable you to leverage the cloud for distributed testing.

## JMeter Cookbook

ISBN: 978-1-78398-828-0        Paperback: 228 pages

70 insightful and practical recipes to help you successfully use Apache JMeter

1. Leverage existing cloud services for distributed testing and learn to employ your own cloud infrastructure when needed.

2. Successfully integrate JMeter into your continuous delivery workflow allowing you to deliver high quality products.

3. Test application supporting services and resources including RESTful, SOAP, JMS, FTP and Database.

Please check **www.PacktPub.com** for information on our titles

open source
community experience distilled

**Learning Internet of Things**

ISBN: 978-1-78355-353-2          Paperback: 242 pages

Explore and learn about Internet of Things with the help of engaging and enlightening tutorials designed for the Raspberry Pi

1.  Design and implement state-of-the-art solutions for Internet of Things using different communication protocols, patterns, C# and Raspberry Pi.

2.  Learn the capabilities and differences between popular protocols and communication patterns and how they can be used, and should not be used, to create secure and interoperable services and things.

**Mapping and Visualization with SuperCollider**

ISBN: 978-1-78328-967-7          Paperback: 222 pages

Create interactive and responsive audio-visual applications with SuperCollider

1.  Master 2D computer-generated graphics and animation

2.  Perform complex encodings and audio/data analysis.

3.  Implement intelligent generative audio-visual systems.

Please check **www.PacktPub.com** for information on our titles

Lightning Source UK Ltd.
Milton Keynes UK
UKOW07f1509130417
299057UK00002B/19/P